Passing t|

Peter Paddon

Passing the Veil

©1996 Peter Paddon

ISBN 1 898307 49 0

Cover design by Daryth Bastin
Cover illustration by Tass

Published by:

Capall Bann Publishing
Freshfields
Chieveley
Berks
RG20 8TF

Contents

Introduction

No book can replace a good teacher, or even membership in a group with more experienced members, but a good book can help the solo practitioner or inexperienced group to head in the right direction. It can also provide enough of the basics to make you a viable proposition to a group when you do find one. That is the aim of this book.

Those of you who read *The Book of the Veil* will be aware of the Sacred Hermetic Order of Asar-Ra (S.H.O.A.R). The chapters of this book are basically the lessons of the correspondence course used by that Order to train newcomers prior to acceptance into a Lodge. They are therefore specifically aimed at those who wish to follow the Egyptian Mysteries, but this does not mean that they will not be of use to anyone else. On the contrary, the basics are applicable to all paths, and while certain small differences may exist - particularly with the interpretation of symbols - the information and exercises given here will be useful for Wiccans, Qabalists, Rosicrucians, and every other type of Western Mystery. Indeed, I know of several Wicca covens who use these lessons as part of their basic training.

The aim of setting up the course was simple - to make available this all-important basic training to as many people as possible. It did not matter that many of them would not enter the Order, or even complete the course. The important thing was to give those who wanted it a chance to get far enough along the path to have something to offer any group they approached. While the course was successful, its reach was limited by the necessity of charging enough to cover administrative costs - resulting in a total cost of about £100 to do the course, though this did include personal tuition and an examination to qualify for Order membership. But not everyone is able to afford £100, even in installments, so the course has been converted into book form, and here it is.

For obvious reasons, the book as a whole is aimed squarely at the novice, but even experienced occultists may find things of use to them in its pages. Several exercises included here have been designed specifically by S.H.O.A.R, and are printed here for the first time, and some of the theory is far from common knowledge, so it is hoped that whatever your level of attainment, you will find something new, something useful here.

Using the lessons

Each chapter in the book is a lesson, consisting of three sections; theory, practical, and homework. It is not essential to work through them in order, though it is recommended as some lessons refer to earlier ones.

Additional notes on the homework exercises have been included in Appendix A. They are there to help you evaluate your own results, and have been placed separately to avoid any influence they might have on your results - think of them as *"teacher's notes"*.

First, read the theory section several times, until you feel that you are familiar with its contents. Then move on to the practical, and reading the instructions as often as needed, try the exercises given, remembering to record your results.

Finally, try the homework exercises several times over the space of a week or two, once again recording your results.

It is important to record your results for several reasons. They will help you to recognise your progress, and will also serve as proof of your work when attempting to join a Lodge/Coven/Group. In addition, if you also record such data as the moon phase, weather, general health, state of mind, and where you are in your menstrual cycle (if you are female), it will enable you to build up knowledge of how conditions around you may affect your magical work.

If you wish to approach S.H.O.A.R for further training, or to affiliate your group with them, write a short letter to the author care of the Publishers, and details will be forwarded to you, but please do not send coursework or queries to the publishers, as they are not in a position to deal with this. This method of contact will involve a delay, so please be patient if you do write.

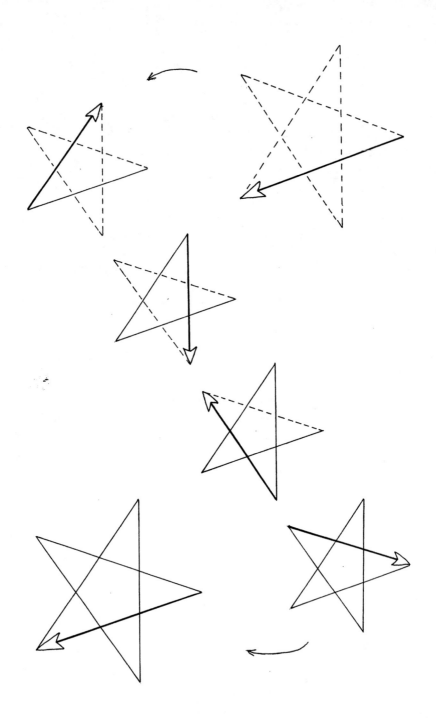

Chapter 1

The Elements

Theory

All forces and influences in the universe can be placed into five categories, which are traditionally referred to as elements. Each of the elements has its own characteristic astral landscape, inhabitants, and correspondences.

Principle of Spirit

The element of Spirit is the causal sphere from which all the other elements are formed. It is the *'Limitless Light'*, the *'Unformed Stuff'* of which written descriptions are of little use. Experience will teach you of its properties, but for now think of it as the material from which astral forms are created.

The Temple officer who corresponds to this element is the Lodge Master, who may or may not be acting as officer of one of the quarters. The Master is the force that binds the disparate elements of the Temple into a whole, and his/her actions and decisions determine the actions of the other officers.

Principle of Fire

Fire is the first element to emerge from Spirit, and is the element of change and transformation. Its appearance in the universe may be likened to the *'Big Bang'* that scientists say started the whole process of Time and Space. Fire, of course, is combustion, and in the physical sense you can see how physical fire transforms whatever it acts upon - toasting bread, roasting meat, converting wood to carbon, and changing chemicals from one compound to another. Its spiritual effect is very similar, though under greater control when used by a trained mind.

Spirit

Fire

Fire is represented in the station of the South, and is called the Gate of the Noonday Sun. Its symbols are the torch, the hammer, the lightning flash, and the Eye of Horus, the Egyptian Godform for this quarter. Its magickal weapon is the wand, for the wand is the power tool of the magician, and fire was originally made by rubbing two sticks together. It is the realm of heroes, including Arthur, Hercules, Gawain, and many others.

The Officer of the South is responsible for the safety of the Temple as its Guardian, both physically and spiritually. The landscape within is in a permanent state of transformation, and it is not wise to travel far in this realm without a guide, such as Michael or Horus, until you are familiar with it.

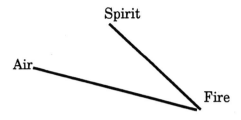

Principle of Air

As the action of Fire (heat) on a chemical produces gas or fumes, so the spiritual element of Fire gives forth the element of Air as a result of its actions. Air is the principle of knowledge and learning, including science, healing, and ritual. We learn from experiences, and any transformation of any type is an experience, both in observation and in being affected.

The station of Air is in the East, and to say that elemental Air is unpredictable is no exaggeration. Its symbols are fans, feathers, wind instruments (especially horns), and all things of an airy nature. Its magickal weapon is the dagger, and this symbolises the magickal knowledge of the magician cutting through the barrier of what is unknown.

The dagger in all its forms represents knowledge - from the scalpel of medicine, through the pen nib of literature, to the ploughshare of efficient agriculture. The Egyptian Godform associated with the East is Osiris, as he was the one who brought civilisation and agriculture to his people. The East is the home of all the teachers of myth, legend and religion; Merlin, Jesus, Buddha, and so on.

The Temple Officer of the East is the Celebrant, whose task in the ritual is to direct the power raised by the rite. He/she sets the pace, guides, directs, and mediates in the role of distributor of communication and knowledge. The inner landscape varies from person to person, but is always similar, being countryside, trees, and blue sky.

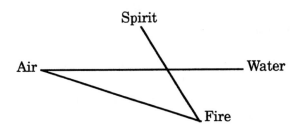

Principle of Water

When a gas, formed by a chemical reaction with heat, moves further away from the source of heat, it cools down and condenses into a liquid at a temperature determined by its atomic structure. In the same way the element of Water condenses out of the element of Air. Water represents emotion, intuition, and psychic abilities, all dependant on prior knowledge.

The Gate of the Setting Sun in the West is the station for Water, and it is here that contacts with the higher planes are made. Its symbols are all receptacles and fluids, and anything of a watery nature. Isis is the godform for this quarter, equating with Artemis, Diana, Hecate, and Astarte. The Officer of the West is the Temple Seer, and is responsible for observing the astral part of the rite and transmitting the power and contacts from there. The landscape is very dreamy and peaceful, often containing a river and waterfall, but always the sound of running water.

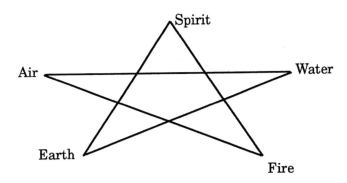

Principle of Earth

Further cooling of a liquid produces a solid, and likewise the element of Water gives way to Earth, solid, stable, and secure. As physical death results in returning to physical earth, so the symbolic death of initiation takes place in the gateway of
Earth.

The final station of the North, the Gate of the Midnight Sun, is the quarter of elemental Earth. It is the place of birth, death, rebirth, and initiation. Its symbols are the horn of plenty, the sickle, the wheatsheaf, the basket, and the scythe. Anubis is the ruling godform, although Geb may be used for nature rites and some lodges use Nephthys to balance the sexual polarity.

The Officer of the North is responsible for setting up the Temple, and for all preparation. Anubis is the guide of the underworld, and it is the duty of the officer to emulate this by undertaking the physical and emotional preparation of the participants of the rite.

Mankind is not popular with the kerubs of Earth, for he rapes the land and exploits its resources. With patience though, you can earn acceptance from them and gain access to their subterranean realm.

The Pentagram

As you have probably noticed, the diagrams in this chapter have traced out a five-pointed star. This symbol, the Pentagram, not only represents the five elements, but is used in ritual to open the Elemental Gateways, for invocation, and for banishing.

Practical

The practical work in this lesson is aimed at gaining experience of the elements through the method of pathworking. Use relaxation techniques to prepare yourself, then visualise the elemental symbol before you. Enlarge it until it is big enough to act as a doorway, then pass through it. Use the following symbols and guidelines, and do not spend too long before returning. Ideally, get your partner to bring you back at a predetermined point, or record a "come back" statement if working solo from a cassette.

Air -*East Blue disk. Landscape bright and airy. Springtime. Trees, Birdsong, Breeze, Blue sky.*

Fire -*South Red triangle, Point up. Landscape volcanic, Changeable, Hot, Summer, Much energy, Possibly stormy sky.*

Water -*West Green or silver crescent, Points up. Landscape fertile, River or Waterfall, Harvest. Autumn, Evergreens. Sunset.*

Earth -*North Yellow square. Landscape deep forest and/or underground. Winter, Night.*

Homework

Do a pathworking to each element in turn, writing your results. It is important to visit the kingdoms in a regular sequence to maintain your own elemental balance. (It does not matter which order you visit them in, only that you use the same order all the time. The important thing is to visit them in equal amounts in order to maintain your own elemental balance). Build up an image in your mind of the landscape described in each section, and meditate on it. What impressions do you get? What do you 'see' that is not mentioned in the descriptions? Record your results.

Chapter 2

Casting The Circle

Theory

There are several questions that need to be answered about circle-casting. This chapter will try to give you some answers.

Why do it ?

There are many reasons for casting a circle when you are doing something of a magickal or psychic nature. Perhaps the most important reason is that using psychic faculties or energies is a sure way of attracting any non-physical entities that may be in the area to yourself, and you therefore need a barrier to keep them out.

Another reason a circle is used is to set a limit to what you are doing, a bit like a resistor in an electronic circuit, or a governor in an engine. Finally, casting a circle sets the space within it apart from the mundane world - it creates a sacred enclosure where men and gods may meet.

What exactly are you doing ?

Casting a circle is an action that takes place on many different levels. On the physical level, you go through the physical act of drawing the circle either on the ground or in the air.

Psychologically, your mind accepts this drawn boundary as being real - you set yourself apart and alter your state of awareness, switch your *'ritual'* mode on. Emotionally, you charge the atmosphere with the sort of sanctity that is found in the great cathedrals, whilst spiritually you create a glowing sphere of light that signals to astral beings that work is to be done, and entrance is by invitation only.

Various ways of casting a circle

Just as drawing a circle on paper can be done with an infinite number of objects - different pens, pencils, pastels; with a pair of compasses, round a plate, with a pin and string - so there are many ways of casting circles for magickal purposes. A powerful circle can be cast by the trained mind with no physical movement at all, purely by visualisation, and even then the options are endless. However, in a practical ritual situation, it is usual to cast the circle physically, either with the fingers or with one of the magickal weapons.

Sometimes a pre-drawn circle is used, sometimes one is marked out on the floor specifically for the work, and sometimes no mark is made physically. It all depends on where you are, what you are doing, what is available, and what your preference is - it is no good drawing out a chalk circle if you don't like using one, or you haven't got any way of making it accurate!

When do you cast a circle ?

The simple answer to this is after you have everything in place, but before you begin your work. Obviously there are occasions when it is unnecessary to cast a circle - you don't need a circle to meditate in, although one will certainly help you to get results. Basically, if any kind of power is being raised, it is a good idea to cast a circle first. If astral *'attack'* is suspected or expected, cast a circle. If you are invoking, evoking, or calling upon any being whatsoever, you should always cast a circle first.

Where do you cast a circle ?

Ideally, you cast it in your own personal temple, but one can be cast just about anywhere. The important thing to remember is that nothing should be inside the circle that could contaminate it, so carpets should be vacuumed, ashtrays, dirty plates and clothing should be removed, and all items not needed for the work should be placed outside the circle. Obviously in an emergency, this would take too long, but wherever possible it should be the rule to *clear* and *clean* a space for working in.

Who casts a circle ?

Anyone can cast a circle, but in a group it is sensible to choose the most proficient circle caster if the work to be done is at all risky or at a high level. Naturally this does not always apply, and the owner of the temple - if there is one - or the group leader may choose someone who would benefit from the practice to cast the circle.

Practical

As mentioned before, circle casting can be done in a variety of ways, and can range from simple visualisation to a complex rite using a variety of tools, incenses and personnel. The first exercise, however, is a simple way of casting a circle that requires no equipment, and is useful for personal protection and experimentation.

The Sphere of Light

This method is one purely of visualisation, and is the simplest way of casting a circle for protection. With practice, it can be done very quickly. Visualise a point of light in the centre of your torso, and when you have it clearly, begin to expand it.

For solo work/protection, make it just big enough for yourself; for groups, let the individual spheres merge and form a large one that fills the room. If one person is forming a sphere for a group, just keep on expanding the sphere until it contains everyone. Once the sphere is in place, being aware of it is enough to keep it in place for a while, although the exercise should be repeated from time to time if extended use is required.

Casting a circle with fingers

The basic ritual circle is cast with the fingers. The index and middle fingers should be extended, with the ring and little fingers tucked into the palm. Place the thumb along the groove between the index and middle fingers. You should use the hand that you find it easiest to push energy through, although traditionally the right hand is used.

Standing in the centre of the workspace, hold your fingers out at shoulder height, arm straight, and turn clockwise. As you do so, visualise a stream of blue light being poured out of the tips of your fingers to '*draw*' the circle. One circle is enough for meditation or divination work, but traditionally for ceremonial work three circuits are used - i. e.., draw the circle three times. In Egyptian Magick this is essential.

Casting a circle with the dagger

Basically, this is the same as when using the fingers, with the exception that the ritual dagger is held in the right hand, and the light that forms the circle is visualised as coming from the point. The dagger is used for all rituals of a non-elemental nature, and for rites of the element of air.

Casting a circle with the wand

Once again, the same technique is used, although the colour of the light from the wand should be red, and is used where the rite is one of a fiery nature, or where strong protection is needed.

Casting a circle with the chalice

Although rarely used, a circle can be cast with a chalice. Rites of a watery nature would benefit from a chalice circle, such as rites for love, or clairvoyance, or divination. The light should be green or silver.

Casting a circle with the pantacle

Casting a circle with the pantacle is a good way of purifying or exorcising a room, and is used where rites of an earthy nature are to be performed. The light should be yellow or gold.

Preparing the space

It is preferable that the area to be worked in should be completely free of all things that may be an avenue for negative entities or vibrations, so where circumstance allows, all debris, dirty clothing or plates, ashtrays, dust, food, and mundane objects must be removed. The floor should be swept/vacuumed, and if necessary, the walls and any needed furniture should be washed down - ideally with a psychic wash solution, but water will do.

Obviously, in an emergency you may find yourself having to cast a circle in a run-down bedsit, in which case you will have to kick, push, or move what you can out of the immediate area of the circle, and be aware of the need to guard against intrusion through what may be left within.

Opening and closing the circle

Once the circle is cast, ideally nobody passes into or out of it until it is dispersed, but for various reasons it is sometimes necessary to let someone through while the circle is in use. In many rites, the circle is cast by one person alone in the room, who then has to admit others. In other circumstances, such as initiations, at a certain stage the candidate has to be fetched, which means that someone has to go and get him/her.

In the Egyptian system, the method of opening a portal is to perform a movement known as *'opening the veil'*. With both arms out in front of you at shoulder height, the backs of your hands touching each other, push your hands apart until they are about door-width apart, visualising a doorway ringed with light the colour of the circle forming as you do so.

The portal is closed by standing with your hands either side of the doorway, palms facing in, and pushing them together until they meet, visualising the doorway becoming narrower as you do so, until when the palms meet the circle is unbroken, and the doorway is no more.

Dispersing the circle

There are two simple ways of dispersing the circle once it is no longer needed. The simplest is to stand cruciform in the centre and say something along the lines of, *"in the name of the Lords of Light I now declare this circle to be dissolved. The rite is ended!"*, clapping your hands together and/or stamping your feet together as you finish saying it. The other way is to *'undraw'* the circle by going anti-clockwise, visualising the light being *'sucked in'* by the fingers or tool. If this method is used, it is vital that you undraw the circle as many times as you drew it originally.

Homework

Practice the various ways of casting a circle, noting your results, and decide which method suits you best. Write a short essay on what the circle symbolises to you.

Chapter 3

Devotions

Theory

You may be asking yourself, *"what are devotions?"* The answer is quite simple. Devotions are the actions you take to identify yourself with a deity or deities, and is a system that by itself will eventually lead to enlightenment - a form of western mental yoga. In practical terms, the Way of Devotion is what you are following when you set up a shrine to deity, and make prayers, offerings, and rites before it as acts of faith.

Why do we do them?

Well, as was mentioned above, they are a pathway to enlightenment, but for the Egyptian magician they are more than that. For members of the S.H.O.A.R it is necessary at a certain stage to take on a deity as a patron, and although you do not need to do so yet, it is important that you understand how to *'treat'* your patron God or Goddess.

Having a strong emotional and spiritual link with a deity has been found to be of great benefit in magical work, and

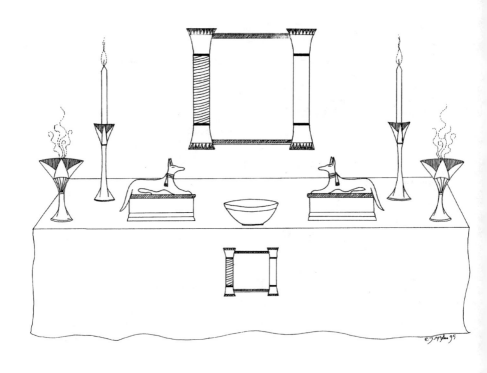

Shrine to a deity

as you progress, you will find many other benefits come to you through your devotions.

So how are devotions carried out?

That is not so easy to answer. Once you have chosen your deity - or they have chosen you! - you must set up a shrine to them, and perform little rites for them. Though there are rules on what is included in the shrine and rites, it is basically down to you. As long as the required items/actions are present, you may do whatever you feel to be right. But note the word *'Devotion'*. It is not chosen lightly. You must develop a close and trusting relationship with your deity in order to benefit - in this area above all, mere lip-service will not bring results, and may well do you harm.

If you set up a shrine - and I hope you do - you must set aside a particular time each day to 'pay your respects'. You do not need to work in a ritual format, although most people choose to. Of course, you can visit your shrine or call upon your deity at any time, but this set-aside time should always be adhered to as closely as possible, as a time to be with - and be one with - your God, rather than a time when you ask for help. A Christian who prays every morning and evening to thank God for his blessings, and prays at odd times for aid, is following the Path of Devotion to his God, although most Christians would vehemently deny they are following *'occult practice'*.

The best place to set up a shrine is in its own room, but this is very rarely practical, so the usual alternative is in your bedroom or somewhere where it is not likely to be disturbed. Sometimes it is impossible to find such a place, and the alternative then is to set aside a surface where you keep just a vase of flowers, keeping your shrine objects in a box to be brought out only when in use. All you need is a small shelf, or the top of a chest of drawers, although ideally you would use a small table that is not ever used for anything else.

Lastly, who do you choose to do your devotions to? The traditional definition is that you choose a godform suited to your own highest nature, but in practice you would choose a godform that you already feel a strong bond with. For that reason, it is very possible that you will have difficulty choosing a godform - you need to experience each one before you can say who you feel best with. Therefore, it is usual in the lower degrees to set up a shrine to Asar-Ra, the patron godform of your Lodge, or to 'The Creator'.

It is not compulsory at this stage to set up a shrine, but it is recommended. It is important, however, to remember that all the Gods and Goddesses named in the various pantheons are aspects of the one Great Un-named Creator.

Practical

The first act of devotion that you would perform within the Lodge is approaching and addressing the Temple altar, which is itself a shrine, not only to Asar-Ra and the Lodge's patron, but to all the adepts who have gone before you in the Egyptian Mysteries, and that is why there is always a lamp lit upon it or above it during any work in the Temple.

Approaching the altar is simple. First, on entering the Temple, place yourself so that you are looking at the altar square-on. Then walk towards it until you are close enough to touch it. Look into the lamp flame, or at the images, and feel with your mind for a unity with the Temple. When you feel ready to work, bow your head gently, and go to your seat. Sometimes visitors will use more elaborate movements, and the Officer of the East and Lodge Master will both touch the altar with their finger-tips when before it, but do not let what others do confuse you. A simple bow of the head is all that is required.

Setting up a shrine

The main item of your shrine should be a figure of the deity - this can be either a statue, a relief, a painting, or a photo of a statue. It should be the best you can afford, or it should be of your own making. Around this image should be placed decorations in keeping with the nature of the godform - symbols, stones, plants, and other representations that correspond to the godform.

There should be a vessel of libation, a wide shallow bowl or chalice, and the altar cloth should have been designed to be harmonious with what the godform stands for.

The power of prayer

It may seem strange to talk of prayer in a magical context, but prayer is a valid technique of contacting your deity, provided that it is performed seriously and sincerely. A very good example of a powerful prayer of devotion is the Song of Isis and Nephthys, which was sung in ancient times in the Temple of Amen-Ra at Thebes as an act of devotion to Osiris:

> *"Hail, thou Lord of the Underworld,*
> *Thou Bull of those who are therein,*
> *Thou image of Ra-Harmachis,*
> *Thou Babe of beautiful appearance,*

Come to us in peace.
Thou didst repel, Thy disasters,
Thou did drive away evil happenings;
Lord, come to us in peace.
O Un-Nefer, Lord of food,
Thou Chief, Thou who art of terrible majesty,
Thou God, president of the Gods,
When Thou dost inundate the land
All things are engendered.
Thou art gentler than the Gods.
The emanations of Thy body make the dead
And the living to live,
O Thou Lord of food,
Thou Prince of green herbs,
Thou Mighty Lord,
Thou staff of life,
thou giver of offerings to the gods,
And of sepulchral meals to the blessed dead.
Thy soul flieth after Ra,
Thou shinest at dawn,
Thou settest at twilight,
Thou risest every day;
Thou shalt rise on the left hand
of Atenu for ever and ever.
Thou art the Glorious One,
the Vicar of Ra; the Company of
the Gods cometh to Thee invoking
Thy face, the flame whereof
reacheth unto Thine enemies.
We rejoice when Thou gatherest
together Thy bones,
and when Thou hast made whole
Thy body daily. Anubis cometh to Thee,
and the Two Sisters (Isis and Nephthys) come to Thee.
They have obtained beautiful things for Thee,
and They gather together

Thy limbs for Thee, and
They seek to put together the
mutilated members of Thy body.
Wipe Thou the impurities which
are on them upon our hair and
come to us having no recollection
of that which hath caused Thee sorrow.
Come Thou in Thy attribute of 'Prince of the Earth,'
lay aside Thy trepidation and be at peace with us,
O Lord. Thou shalt be proclaimed heir
of the world, and the One God, and the Fulfiller
of the Designs of the Gods.
All the Gods invoke Thee,
come therefore to Thy Temple
and be not afraid. O Osiris,
Thou art beloved of Isis and Nephthys;
rest Thou in Thy habitation forever ".

(Budge, The Book of the Dead, Dover)

Homework

Write a prayer to your concept of the Creator, and design on
paper a shrine for Him/Her/It.

Chapter 4

Raising Power

Theory

There are several types of energy to be found within the human body, all of which are to some extent used in magick. The first - and most obvious - is electrical energy. It has been a well-known fact in the scientific world for decades that the physical body runs on electricity; electrical impulses carry messages along our nerves, transmit instructions through and from the brain, and trigger off the muscle actions that enable us to move, breathe, and live. There is therefore a weak but physically detectable electronic field around the body.

Another type of energy generally accepted as present in the body is magnetic energy. The blood contains iron, and there are various other metallic elements to be found in minute quantities throughout the rest of the body - gold in human hair, for example. These metallic traces combine to produce a magnetic field that is visible in Kirlian photography.

Where there are electrical and magnetic energies, it is not surprising to find electromagnetic energies, and in an electrically operated mechanism made of carbon compounds impregnated with traces of metals, it would be strange not to find such forces. The electromagnetic field around the body is not generally detectable by scientific means, but many physicists have postulated its existence.

In magickal terms it equates to what is known as the etheric form of the body, and is detectable psychically as a blue-white hazy light extending approximately one inch from the skin.

Finally, there is the life-force, odic force, or astral bodies. These are bodies of subtle energy, not detectable by normal means, which create the psychic effect known as the aura.

It is a law of physics that all changes require energy of a relevant type in order for them to happen. You can not expect water to turn to steam without the application of energy in the form of heat. So it is that each of the above energies is used in specific ways to achieve results in magick. To create a change in yourself, you would make use of the electrical energy within you.

An example is an esoteric way of dieting; by training yourself to visualise your glands secreting fat-digesting endorphins - normally produced when you eat fewer carbohydrates than you are burning up - you stimulate the flow of electrons to the relevant glands and actually do produce the endorphins. By conditioning yourself to produce them whenever you eat, you substantially increase the rate of weight-loss. Likewise, ailments caused by a body disfunction can be remedied by visualisation techniques (Such as those now being used to aid cancer patients).

Another way electrical and magnetic energy can be used within the body is in healing of viral or germ-caused disease. This type of illness will cause an imbalance in the energy field around the affected area due to the intrusion of the energy field of the germs or viruses. Visualisation of increased energy flow of the relevant type will quickly clear these infections up. You will have realised by now that visualisation is the key to using energy.

Electromagnetic energy, and to a lesser extent electrical and magnetic energies, can be extended outside the limits of the body and used to alter the metabolism of others. Most psychic healing is of this nature, and the effect ranges from the basic results obtained by general healing techniques to spectacular results when a well-trained and experienced healer is at work. Electromagnetic energy can be used to affect your immediate environment, though usually through the agency of living organisms. The *'Odic Force'* that comprises the astral body is much more far-reaching in its effect. This energy is used by visualising a desired outcome on the astral and then ritually *'earthing'* it to the material world. It does not require the intervention of other life-forms, and is not confined by either time or space.

All ritual is basically the control of this force; concentration aids for fine-tuning the specific vibrations of energy and pin-point targeting. There are, of course, two sources of energy for magical use; that which is within the body, and that which is within every thing in the universe, popularly known as Cosmic energy.

For healing purposes, energy from within is usually sufficient, but a magician will almost always *'charge up'* with energy from the world around him/her in order to obtain better results from his/her rituals. Once again, this can be of a general nature, or a charge of one specific vibration can be raised.

Practical

As you learnt in the theory section, the key to using power is visualisation. Starting with the energy naturally present in the body, let us look at how to guide it with visualisation.

The main thing to remember about energies is that they are all identical except for one thing - rate of vibration. The colours of the spectrum are merely energy at different rates of vibration; sound is yet another rate, as are radio wavelengths. This makes the art of controlling energy by visualisation very simple, as all energy has a colour when observed psychically. This means that in order to control the flow of electrical energy within your body, you should visualise it as a glowing red flow going where you want it to. Try it now; visualise a stream of red light flowing from your solar plexus to your right hand. Very quickly you will feel the build up of energy in your hand. Magnetic energy is blue, and electromagnetic energy white or pale blue.

In a darkened room, you will find with practice that you can actually 'see' the energy within and around your body, if you look slightly out of focus - look past your hand rather than directly at it. It will not necessarily work first time, so keep trying. Once you can 'see' the energy - electromagnetic is the easiest - you will find that you can make the white light go further from your body than the red or blue. This is because the electromagnetic field, though weaker than the electrical or magnetic fields, has a more extended effect due to its subtler vibrations.

As you practice, you will find that you begin to see the colours of your aura, and visualisation will control the flow of those energies too. Now is the time to visualise drawing in energy from outside your body - but concentrate your efforts on white and gold light only for the time being. You will find after a while that you can draw energy in and concentrate it in or around any part of your body very strongly. White energy drawn in and then added to a little red or blue energy from within will take on the colour you add, and this is how you 'charge' for an extra-strong healing effect.

You will have noticed that when you draw in energy through your hands there is a difference in the 'feel' of the energy, depending on what your hands are aimed at. If you experiment, you will find that with practice you will be able to differentiate between living and dead organic objects, minerals, crystals, metals, and synthetic materials by the feel of the energy they emit. This can be quite a useful ability, and can be developed to a very fine level.

There are several exercises that can increase sensitivity to the energies. A selection are given below.

Tactile - palm
Try rubbing your palms together briskly, then *"feeling"* for an energy source. The friction *"wakes up"* the nerve endings in the palm and makes them more sensitive.

Tactile - fingertips
Tapping the fingers of each hand upon the the thumb tips in sequence as fast as possible has a similar effect as the first exercise but limited to the fingertips.

Visual - one
Gaze straight ahead with your thumbs at arm's length before you focus on your thumbs. Without

refocussing your eyes, move your thumbs to either side nand see how far apart they can get while still "seeing them". Keep it up for at least a minute, swining your thumbs centre to sides. This wakes up the subtle senses.

Visual - two

When looking at the object you wish to examine, gaze slightly above and to the right and focus on something beyond the object so that the object is out of focus to your physical sight. After a few minutes you will become aware of a field of distortion around the object which with practice will be seen to be coloured.

Homework

Practice the techniques described and report your results. Experiment with how you sense different forms of energy, and record your results.

Chapter 5

Temple Visualisation

Basic

Theory

In some magickal working groups there is a great emphasis on study, but little or no instruction on the actual metaphysical mechanics of the Temple rite. New members are told the physical moves, given a few general rules, and are then left to discover the inner workings of the temple by a form of psychic osmosis. This is akin to putting a teenager behind the wheel of a car on his seventeenth birthday, giving him a few pointers on the highway code, and letting him figure out how to drive for himself. Unfortunately, the results are often the same in both cases.

There are two important keys to the Egyptian rites, the Word, and the Image. Of the two, the first one to be learnt is the Image - i. e., visualisation. This encompasses much more than visualising the circle and the beings invoked, as the Temple has its non-physical aspects that need to be acknowledged, as well as the astral participants of the rite, the Lords of the Four Quarters, guardians, etc.

As you learnt in the last chapter, visualisation is an important tool for controlling energies. For general purposes colour alone suffices, but in a full ritual you are looking for more than the presence of a particular form of energy - you are seeking the presence of the archetype that governs the force. This, when done correctly, results in a clearer, purer, and stronger presence of that force, and its use is facilitated by the archetype in a way that no other method would permit.

Traditionally, the images visualised by the adepts within the Temple were the hidden keys to the system, and over centuries of use these images became charged with an immense power. The Lodges of S.H.O.A.R are specifically named after places that contained a Temple of the Four Orders which had used and built up an astral counterpart containing these power-charged images. Using those same images within the new Temple re-aligns them with it and gives them all the power of the original, and for that reason all students of the Order learn them as they progress through the grades.

The visualisations consist of many different levels; the godforms, the watchtowers, the circle itself, and perhaps most important of all, the astral structure of the Temple itself and everything in it. It is this last aspect that we shall deal with in this lesson, as it is a vital part of being an effective member of the Lodge.

The word "temple" originally referred to a cleared space for making observations. Usually on a hilltop, these temples took time and trouble to reach, and the climb left the seeker in need of rest, which placed him or her in a receptive state of passivity ideal for inner realm contacts.

In the modern Temple it is necessary to provide an artificial environment to stimulate and strengthen spiritual abilities. The Temple symbolises the ideal human individual, and everything within it has a special meaning which should be comprehended by all using the Temple. This comprehension must be gained by experiencing the symbols. Seeing the sword should evoke a feeling of keenness and being sharp-witted to a point, the wand should evoke feelings of uprightness, and so on. The first step towards this comprehension is the conscious adoption of the correct behavioural procedures at all levels, as follows:

Body

All bodily behaviour should be dedicated to establishing contacts with deity. This includes ingesting symbolic substances, moving around the Temple, breathing, awareness of the physical surroundings. These areas, covered in a later lesson, have a profound initial effect, but acclimatisation diminishes this effect.

Mind

All stimuli of a purely mental or intellectual nature are included here. The spoken word, and the interpretation of visual images is an important area of this process, which is the mainstay of the experienced student. The techniques involved require the recipient to be capable of being in harmony with the process, and the effect of the techniques increases with experience. S.H.O.A.R places great emphasis on the lessons concerning how to provide these stimuli.

Soul

These procedures seek a response on an emotional level. Physical symbols, music, incense, and colours are the important factors, triggering either an instinctive or conditioned emotional response.

Spirit

The animating principle of all human individuals, spirit is alive in us to experience itself through all we think or do as conscious creatures. The Temple is a nexus where the principles of body, mind, and soul interact to serve the spirit. It is only when the other three are functioning in harmony that Spirit can come into its own and provide the necessary inner contact.

It should be obvious by now that the members of the Temple are part of the symbolism, and for that reason, selection is strict. In order to be accepted into the Temple you must show yourself to be committed to the basic beliefs of the Order, and be willing and able to participate in the practices of the Order, and so you undergo a probationary period prior to initiation.

In addition to representing the perfected human, the Temple also represents the spiritual structure of the universe. Although physically rectangular, the Temple is perceived spiritually as a sphere divided into four segments.

The true Temple is itself a state of consciousness, and the symbolism of the physical Temple acts as an *"autopilot"* to get us to a specific goal, which is the central theme of the

Temple. An understanding of the various symbols is built up gradually by experiencing them individually and together.

Practical

Symbol conditioning, the work of developing an understanding of the symbols, is possible by attending sufficient rites in the Temple, but it is best to practice at home until it becomes second nature first, as greater benefit can then be drawn from the rites. This could be done by drawing them on paper and meditating about them, but it is much better to use a set of symbols, either full-size or miniatures, that can be easily handled. It is important to be conversant with the significance of each symbol before doing the exercise with it, and the three examples given here indicate the level of depth. In future lessons on particular symbols or items, it will be assumed that this exercise is to be carried out at home with them.

The Crown

Assumption of this symbol signifies reaching an arrival at the apex of anything.

There is a peak of achievement that cannot be surpassed by a human, although this varies from person to person and with time.

The crown signifies the maximum that you can attain at any given instant. In the Order the usual headdress is the nemyss. When spelt *"nemmes"*, this means enlightenment, so by assuming it, you take it to represent your most spiritual self, and putting it on signifies that you are striving for that achievement. The wearing of a crown by the Master at initiations has the same meaning, plus the striving for the leadership ability of Osiris as a great teacher and inspirer.

The crown rests on our head, and draws our attention to the crown chakra, through which divine energy and enlightenment enters us *"from above"*. Humans have always instinctively felt that divinity is *"up there"*, and so we direct ourselves towards the light with face raised upwards. The ornament of a headdress, crowning the part of us that is nearest the heavens signifies the rulership of righteousness, which should control our conduct as creatures of the cosmos.

The nemyss should be held before you with both hands on the headband. Starting with the hands close together, the view resembles that of the female sex organ, hinting at the wonders and mysteries of life emerging from the womb of nature. Opening the band out to view the empty interior of the nemyss suggests the brain empty of worthwhile thoughts. Placing it firmly on your head with both hands and adjusting it calls to mind the responsibility it represents, plus a feeling that only special thoughts should occupy the mind while wearing it. Remove it and think of trivialities, replace it and think only sacred thoughts. Repeat this until it becomes automatic.Then try without the nemyss, but with visualisation and the hand movements, them purely with visualisation.

A good passage to say or think while assuming the nemyss is:

> *"I am putting this on my head not to make me look important but to demonstrate by a practical action that I am willing to rule myself as I believe You*

require. If I am right, then assist me, and if I am wrong, correct me. In either case, guide me. I realise that self-rulership is a responsibility I must accept and a burden I must bear with honour if I ever intend to become any higher than a human being. Spirit of Life and Light, crown my consciousness with the illumination of Understanding Wisdom."

The Cube

In theory, this is what you are standing on in the Temple, because it is the firmest foundation of your faith, based on rock-solid ground. In practice, this signifies the floor of the Temple and the sandals on your feet. Factually, it is the feeling of firmness between your feet and the floor. The cube is assumed to be composed of six solid pyramids with their points meeting in the centre.

Masonically, the black and white squares found on some temple floors represent black and white cubes, the black representing the rough ashlar, ordinary men, and the white representing the finished ashlar, or perfected man. These finished ashlars fit together perfectly without any mortar, and so the members of the Lodge should fit together, bonded by spiritual love.

The cube represents having your basic faith supporting you, and it thus becomes obvious why you must accept the basic beliefs of the Order in order to be effective. If you can not accept with certainty, accept a temporary set of workable beliefs as a *"working hypothesis"* until experience leads you to a more permanent set.

In this way you end up with a path towards enlightenment composed of stepping stones, some firmer than others, but all leading you towards a solid foundation on which to build your own inner temple.

Planting your feet firmly on the floor, visualise your beliefs as clearly as you can, and think along the lines of

> *"here stand I, I can do no other. This is what I firmly believe at present, and only the very best reasons could make me change that. It supplies my faith in life and gives me grounds for basing myself on what I feel is spiritually solid enough to last my lifetime. As my feet have to support my body, so does my belief support my soul. May I always find some good grounds wherever I may wander through the ways of living and serving Supreme spirit."*

Your cube symbol should have your creed engraved or marked on it. A creed is a spiritual standpoint represented by the cube, and can be condensed into a symbol such as the rose cross, solar disk, symbol of the Order, or whatever. The creed could be recited while treading a pattern on the floor, or tapping the feet.

The Star

This most significant symbol has an ideology beyond human understanding. Essentially it symbolises the central *"Light Within"* which motivates humanity. Its physical symbols are the Temple lamp, and the lamen worn over the heart.

This lamen, whether it be degree symbol, badge of office, or personal symbol, typifies the Inner Light as experienced by the wearer, and for that reason should be made by the wearer.

Place the star or lamen around your neck, and light the Lamp or a candle before you, and say:

> *"This emblem signifies my spiritual origin and hoped-for end in eternity. If humanity came from the stars in the first place and must eventually return there, then let this symbol stand for my inner instinct that enlightens me on this quest and guides me onwards. I know that if I follow this faculty faithfully enough, it will lead me to the ultimate aim I seek, for it cannot do otherwise.This symbol is a light that represents the divine spark within me, a god-glow. Sometimes it may be bright and at other times feeble, but as long as it shines at all it will ensure my spiritual safety. It is literally the Light of my Life. It and I are one."*

Homework

Practice the exercises given in the practical section, giving your results. For the crown you may construct a nemyss or use any soft hat such as a skullcap, a beret, or a baseball cap, providing it is clean - either new or freshly washed.

Chapter 6

Pathworking

Theory

Pathworking is a fairly new term for what used to be called *'Scrying in the Spirit Vision'*, a term that is heavily dated, and not very accurate. It is a subjective experience, projecting the mind/self into a series of situations, landscapes, and events that can either be observed on a mental level, or with training experienced as a participant with full sensory perception.

As mental observation, pathworking is a form of controlled daydream, though a very effective tool for preparing for a situation or bringing about psychological changes within yourself. As an occult technique backed up by proper training, it is a very potent tool for the magician, but carries its own risk, that of obsession or *'Glamour'*. There is a danger that the subjective world visited may grow too real for those who find it difficult to cope with the 'real' world. Properly used, pathworkings can stretch and improve your knowledge, capability, and not least your imagination, but they are addictive to a weak will, and in extreme cases can lead to a withdrawal from the real world.

But what are we doing when we use pathworkings? Basically, we are using creative visualisation to follow a predetermined path through a series of connected concepts, symbols, or events, presented in the form of a journey. In pathworking, we are trying to *get off the ground* and extend ourselves into Inner Dimensions by pushing ourselves up between a dual concept, which is our intention and our goal.

Each concept is like the side of a ladder, and we bring them as close to us as possible so that we can ascend the ladder by using the steps/stages between them. An important part of the technique is to develop an unwavering concentration, of the kind we would have when crossing a narrow bridge over a dangerous chasm.

The principle of pathworking is not unlike squeezing a tube of toothpaste. When you remove the cap and apply pressure to the sides of the tube, the paste can only go one way - out. By imposing the limits of the chosen principles on ourselves, removing the *'cap'* of restrictions, distractions, etc, and applying the pressure of concentration, our consciousness is forced up onto a higher level. Obviously, this is an exercise that gets better with practice.

For the student new to pathworking, there is a variety of techniques to assist the concentration. Many basic pathworkings have an obvious dual symbolism to accentuate the necessary subtle one - images of forked paths, twin pillars, a hood limiting the view on both sides, etc., and further help can be gained from two-tone chanting, or a double-beat rhythm - a very effective aid to pathworking is to play a recording of a human heartbeat in the background, as this also tends to relax us as well as being a double-beat that is intrinsically linked to our psyche. Reduced to its simplest terms, pathworking is taking two preconditioned factors of consciousness, associating them so as to produce a calculated result, and then continuing the line of pressure into a different dimension of awareness.

There are two basic types of pathworking, both suited to different purposes. The first, under full control, consists of a whole journey, mapped out for the *'traveller'* either on paper, tape, or spoken live by an instructor or partner. Each step of the journey is carefully set out, and responses are controlled by the narrative. Usually sufficient *'blanks'* are left to enable the students progress in the technique as well as the path to be gauged by the things those blanks are filled with. The second type of pathworking is the passive or open pathworking. In this method the traveller is taken to a certain point, then journeys onward from that point alone. This technique, which should not be attempted until you are competent with the first method, may be terminated by a controlled return at a preset time, guided by the instructor, or the student is left to make the return in his/her own time. The latter is best left for the very experienced student.

Practical

The first step in effective pathworking is to relax properly. Ideally, you will be sitting in a comfortable chair, or on the floor if you are comfortable there. It is not recommended that you lie on the floor or a bed at first, as until you have become familiar with the technique you may fall asleep instead of travelling, especially if you have had an exhausting day! The best way to relax is to take a few deep breaths, then proceed to deliberately relax each muscle by mentally commanding it to relax as you first tighten, and then release it. You may work either from head down to feet, or feet up to head, but try to attend to them in sequence, as this minimises the re-tensing of muscles, and ensures that you relax all of them.

Once you have relaxed the body, you must relax the mind, and this is best done by breathing. Using a count of four, you can do this quite easily. Breathe in for eight counts slowly, hold for four, then breathe out for eight, and hold the lungs empty for four counts. The count can be taken from your heartbeat, an external rhythm, or an audio source.

The next stage is to enter the state of awareness required for pathworking. An effective mental journey can be obtained without this stage, but for maximum benefit, this is an important part of the exercise. Choose an abstract symbol and visualise it as strongly as you can. It does not need to be a symbol that has a specific meaning - indeed, if it does have a meaning, it should be relevant to the pathworking at hand, or to the act of pathworking. See it clearly, and focus your attention fully on the symbol, then banish it - will it to vanish. You will be left with a state of empty expectance, known as the *'hole in space'*, and are ready to begin the pathworking.

Before we go into the exercises, a brief word on your physical position. The most important thing to do is to have the spine straight. A kneeling posture like the Arthurian knights at their vigil is suitable, or the sitting position of the Egyptian Gods, with the forearms along the thighs and feet square upon the floor. When lying down, clasp the hands over the solar plexus. Pathworking can be done in a standing position, the best being with one foot at right angles and immediately behind the other, the hands held palm to palm with fingers pointing up, over the region of the heart.

Finally, earthing yourself after the exercise is as important for a pathworking as for a ritual, and can be done as follows. You must make a realisation of your outer life identity by saying either out loud or mentally something like:

> *"My name is so and so, I am a so forth, living at such and such address. I have had an Inner experience that will help me express this Outer Being to better effect. Now I am coming back to my ordinary self improved by what I have just seen."*

If you stamp your foot on the ground as you say/think this, you will program yourself so that the action will produce the return to a normal state of awareness. Where work is done within a circle, this should be done before leaving the circle, and in all cases you should eat something afterwards.

The Beginning of the Journey

(This pathworking should be used in the manner described above. Get your partner to read it to you, or record it on cassette and play it back to yourself. Remember to record your impressions afterwards.)

You find yourself standing on a stone quayside on a riverbank. The river is the Nile, wide and sedate. In the water is a boat with a ferryman at the oars. As you look at the boat, you see your reflection in the water, and notice that you are dressed in the white robe and panther skin of a Priest of Khem.

You climb into the boat, and the ferryman rows you across the Nile to the far bank. As the boat nudges against the quay, you step onto the land, and begin to walk toward the mountains some distance away. You feel within you a sense of vibration, and can hear with your mind's ear the music of a small harp.

Finally you reach the mountains, and follow a narrow track that leads through the mountain range. As you progress the mountains loom ever higher above you on either side, and the pathway becomes dark and cold as you walk on ground that the sun never warms with its rays.

You make your way through ever increasing blackness, starting at every sound as if you were a rabbit, fearful and cold. But still you hear the faint lyre-music from within, and it spurs you on. Despite the cold, despite the stiffness in your limbs that makes you feel as unbending as a roll of papyrus, until you realise that it is getting lighter, and warmer, and you realise that you have made it to the other side of the mountain.

The walk through the corridor of darkness has cleansed you, and though you still feel as if you are made of papyrus, it is as if you were a roll bound by a red cord, signifying that the contents of your "scroll" are important, true, and free from malice. Clear of the mountain range now, you pause at a crystal lake to wash the dust from your feet, and feel the ache of your limbs flowing away as they are cleansed by the water. Now you feel rested and pure.

By the pool, you discover a small herd of seven goats who begin to follow you as you walk towards a temple at the top of a small hill. Upon reaching the temple, you pass between the two great pillars of the portal, and a priest steps out of the shadows and leads the goats away. A priestess leads you to the sanctuary at the heart of the temple, and from a pouch at your waist you take an offering of cake, grain, and incense and place it upon the offering table. You begin to speak words of thanks for the safe journey, and are surprised to see that as your words leave your lips, they are transformed into butterflies that fly to the statue of the deity and perch there. You smile, realising that your journey across the Nile and through the mountains was worthwhile.

The Priestess brings you a small honey cake and a flat loaf of bread, and as you eat them, you smell the sweet scent of the incense being burnt for the gods. You are given a flask of water for the return journey, and a staff upon which is a rayed star, and you leave the temple to return. This time, as you walk through the mountains, you find that the cold does not affect you, and the star on your staff radiates enough light to enable you to see your way with ease. You finally reach the bank of the Nile as the sun sets, and as the ferryman rows you back across the river, you see the bright star in the southern sky, gleaming like a hawk's eye, as all fades, and you return to your physical self.

Homework

Do the pathworking several times, noting your reactions and impressions each time. Pay particular attention to anything that you see that is not described by the text.

Chapter 7

Attributes of the Gods

Theory

No one who strolls through the Egyptian galleries of a museum can fail to be struck by the multitude of divinities who attract attention on all sides. Colossal statues in sandstone, granite, and basalt, minute statues in ceramic, bronze, and gold, portray gods and goddesses in hierarchical poses, seated or standing. They can be seen in the reliefs and decorations of stelae, sarcophagus, papyrus, and wall, receiving adoration and offerings, or performing services for their worshippers.

With this multitude of deities on show, it may seem strange to affirm that the majority of ancient Egyptians - certainly all of the priesthood - believed firmly in the One God, but this fact is proven time and time again by references to the One God, the Creator, the Great Unnamed Creator, and various other terms not ascribed to any named deity. Each deity is at some time referred to as the One God, but none of the other terms is used for a named god. The use of the term 'the One God' has been used by Christian scholars - where it has not been ignored - as a proof of the invalidity of all such terms, because of its use for so many deities.

What they failed to recognise was that it was used in the sense of *'Aspect of the One God'*, which is what the priests believed their gods and goddesses to be. Each deity in the Egyptian Mysteries was considered on three levels.

Firstly, the legend of that deity was a lesson on many levels. Some set an example of right living, some showed the result of wrong living, while others gave explanations for natural phenomena - but they all had inner meanings to the initiates, lessons of spiritual progress and magical power when properly interpreted. The deity also stood as an embodiment of the force that it represented, for example, Isis was the embodiment of protection and healing.

The gods were mediators with the Creator, much as Christ, the Apostles, and Saints mediate with God on behalf of the Christian. And lastly, they were all part of the Creator, parts that could be comprehended and communicated with. The Creator was too vast, too all-encompassing, too impersonal for any but the most adept of men to contact, so the priests of antiquity used their arcane skills to differentiate the forces of order and chaos into the archetypes that we now recognise as deities. They did this by recognising the fact that the whole was made from parts, much as a musical chord is made up of individual notes, or the spectrum of light of different colours, and giving form to those parts.

This did not involve any arbitrary *'design'* exercise, but each type of force, or energy was contacted, not once, but many times, and the force itself resolved into a particular form as it filtered through the consciousness of the priests, and the archetypes thus formed gained solidity and strength from the rites and exercises involved.

Thus, through the agency of man, the Gods created themselves - a fact remembered in the various creation myths of the world. The archetypes, at first subjectively existing in the minds of the priests, gave the priests their true names and called themselves into objective existence. Now is perhaps a good time to look briefly at some of the major deities of the Mysteries. The Gods were arranged in a variety of hierarchical orders, the greatest being the Greater Company of Gods, rules by Ra or an aspect of Him, such as Amun-Ra, or Ra-Herachty - known to us as Asar-Ra, which was his Secret name, only used in the sanctuary by the adepts of His Temple. A working knowledge of all the major gods was essential to the priests and magicians, and they could all be encountered in the magical universe by a suitably qualified magician.

Anubis

The guide and protector within the magical universe, He is shown with the body of a man and the head of a dog - not a jackal as is commonly believed, but of the hunting hounds of the pharaoh. He was the son of Osiris and Nephthys, and step-brother to Horus.

Hathor

The consort of Horus, she is usually shown as a woman with a solar disk enclosed in cows horns, and sometimes as a cow. Goddess of music and love, She is the personification of fertile space, and strongly linked with Nuit.

Horus

Son of Isis and Osiris, and the avenger of His father. He is shown as a hawk, or as a man with a hawk's head, and is the personification of the Sacred Warrior and solar initiator.

Isis

Wife and sister of Osiris and mother of Horus. She is Mistress of the Words of Power, and Goddess of Nature. Shown as a woman with a throne-shaped headdress, She is the embodiment of nature and magick, ruling over the processes of solidification.

Khepera

The Rising Sun, He is shown as a Scarab, or as a man with a Scarab for a head, and is the God of Transformation. KhnemuRam-headed god of creation, He is the Potter who forms our material bodies on his wheel, and who purifies our souls in His kiln. He wears the White crown with a pair of horns, a pair of plumes, and the solar disk.

Maat

Wife of Thoth and daughter of Ra, She represents law and justice, and is the personification of karma. She is shown as a woman with a single white feather as her headdress. As dispenser of rewards and punishments, She is known as the Double Maati. ("the Two Truths")

Nephthys

Daughter of Geb and Nuit, and sister of Isis, Osiris, and Set, her headdress is the hieroglyph for 'Lady of the House', though it is commonly referred to as a basket. She rules over all processes of dispersion.

Nu

His name means 'the Waters of Heaven', and He is the watery abyss out of which all life came. He is the Father of Manifestation.

Nuit

She is the mother of Osiris, Isis, Nephthys, and Set, and as Goddess of the Sky she is usually shown naked arched over the earth. Esoterically She is infinite space, and is called Goddess of the Night Sky in Her role of feminine initiator. Her husband is Geb, the Earth.

Osiris

The God of the Dead, Judgement, and Rebirth. Son of Geb and Nuit, Husband of Isis. Usually shown as a green faced mummy wearing the White Crown, He was originally the God of grain and vegetation. His name means 'That which Reincarnates', and he is connected with the solar and lunar currents of magick.

Ptah

The Lord of Life, one of the oldest Gods. He is a highly creative architect, and the human body was designed by Him. He is shown as a bearded man wearing a skullcap and swathed in bandages, from which His hands project.

Ra

The ultimate personification of the solar current, He is depicted as a hawk-headed man bearing the double crown, and is highly creative.

Geb

The God of the Earth, he is shown as a crowned human or as the Goose that laid the World Egg.

Sekhmet

The Goddess of magick and retribution, She is depicted as a woman with the head of a lioness and the solar disk and uraeus upon Her head. The personification of all feminine and female principles, She is a teacher and initiator, but her lessons are not easy.

Set

Brother and slayer of Osiris, He is equal in power to Horus, and opposes creativity, representing darkness and the desert. He is shown as a man with the head of a mythical creature with a curved snout and squared off ears. He is the current of magick that opposes all manifestation in matter, i. e., Chaos.

Shu

Son of Ra and Hathor, brother of Tefnut, He separated the Sky, Nuit, from the Earth, Geb, and is shown as a man with a feather or double feather headdress. One of the Guardians of the Gate of Heaven.

Tefnut

Twin sister of Shu, She is moisture and the creative power of sunlight. A female with the head of a lioness with an uraeus headdress, she is also a Guardian of the Gate of Heaven.

Tem

The Setting Sun, he is shown as a man wearing the double crown, and is the Bringer of Dreams.

Thoth

The God of Wisdom, He gave man language and was Himself a Scribe for the Gods. He is shown with the head of an Ibis, sometimes with an ape by his side. He was the husband of Maat, and His role is to record all the words spoken and deeds done on earth for each person, so that Osiris may use it to judge them.

There are, of course, other deities both major and minor, but these are a good introductory selection.

Practical

The best way to learn about the Gods and Goddesses of Egypt is to experience them, and outside of ritual there are two effective ways of doing this. When you are familiar with the image of a deity, you may visualise that image before you, and work as in a pathworking, or assume the stance of the deity and visualise yourself as that image. This does require a degree of skill, however, particularly if you are assuming the image of one of the less pleasant deities.

The second method is simpler and safer. It involves visualising the name or symbol of the deity before you, and breathing it into your body, and then meditating on it. It is important to visualise breathing it out again and dispersing it after the exercise, in order to avoid being glamourised, or 'possessed'. Ideally, the exercise is approached in the same way as a pathworking, and can even take place in an astral environment.

It is useful to visualise the name or symbol in the relevant colour if possible, although a general turquoise or Isis blue can be used effectively for all deities. Each deity you come across should be experienced in this way. If you feel you want to use the image method, you should if possible have a partner working with you, so that you can be talked out of difficulties.

When working with a partner in either exercise, questions and answers can be used to draw information out, and the partner can keep notes. When working solo, notes should be made immediately after finishing, as the nature of the information received is very transient, and will be quickly lost if not fixed by writing it down.

For this session, we will practice with four of the deities: Osiris, Isis, and Horus for their good effects. Set, the most dangerous deity to encounter, should be met only with assistance from an experienced partner.

Osiris - colours, green and white, metal, gold, symbol, the column.

Isis - colour, turquoise blue, metal, silver, symbol, throne.

Horus - colour yellow, metal gold, symbol, Eye of Horus.

Homework

Use the name/symbol method to explore and experience deities, recording your results and impressions.

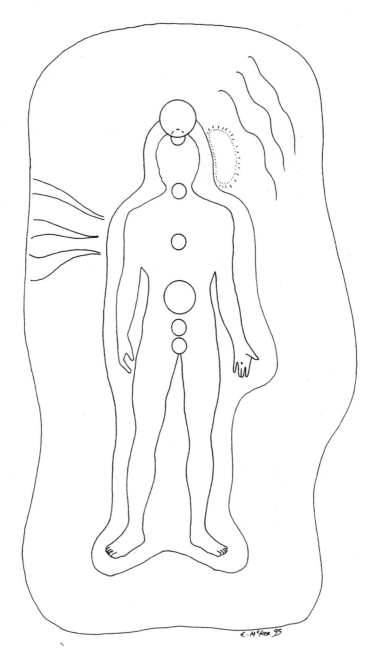

The aura

Chapter 8

Healing

Theory

Throughout the ages there has been no area of magick or religion that has been given more interest than that of healing. Almost every *'miracle'* of legend, holy scripture, and folklore is concerned with the healing of some person or persons.

The desire of mankind to cure self and loved ones led to supplications to the deities for intervention, and modern orthodox religions continue to do this in the form of prayers. However, for the magician priests of the ancient world, this was too passive a method, and guided by their gods, their own intuition, and good fortune, two paths of healing art developed.

The first was the use of plants and minerals to treat ailments. While this was in the hands of the priesthood treatment was holistic, and fruitful. But as the treatment of illness became a specialisation, it became more divorced from spiritual practice, and gradually the medical practitioners became separated from the priesthood. This in turn led to a loss of the spiritual aspect of diagnosis, and patients began to be treated for their symptoms.

Naturally, the plants and extracts in use were not as efficient in this way, and the doctors refined and refined them over the centuries until today they prescribe chemicals so potent that they will cure the symptom targeted, but the dose must be within tight limits to prevent side-effects and even death. A modern move towards more holistic treatment is causing a resurgence in herbal and related treatments, which are slower to act due to being targeted at the cause and not the symptom, but just as certain and free from side-effects when prescribed correctly.

The second path of healing has always remained locked firmly with spiritual teachings, and that is the direct manipulation of aura and energies to combat imbalances, often before any physiological symptoms show. In the modern world the work is carried mainly by spiritualist healers, though they are often working from intuition rather than from formal training. It is the hope that these lessons on healing will provide that formal training.

The first question to be answered is *'why does spiritual healing work?'* The answer lies in the phenomenon known as the aura. The various areas of the aura tell us many things. Within the egg-shaped aura several patterns can be seen; the glowing spheres of the chakras or energy centres, the vertical striations of colours denoting personality, and the horizontal striations, often moving, denoting emotions. All of these can reveal a lot about the patient, his/her state of mind, spirituality, etc., but for the purpose of healing, two things are of greatest importance.

Firstly, striations around the head will indicate a psychological condition - many illnesses have a psychological foundation - while patches of muddy colour, discolouration, and the dark greys and browns, will indicate where physiological problems are present or imminent. It is a well known fact that two complimentary colours will cancel themselves out, and this is precisely how colour healing works, by visualising the complementary colour over the affected area. This is however a crude method, though it does demonstrate how healing works, by using a controlled energy input to neutralise an uncontrolled pattern of energy that is either the cause or the result of a problem. It hardly bears stating that this is still a quite symptomatic form of treatment, but the answer is one of refinement, not redirection.

By learning to read the aura in depth with great accuracy, the healer can develop the skill to interpret the inter-relation of colours, energies, and patterns within the patient. A particular disorder may be seen to be caused by elements in the aura *'attracting'* the energy type that triggers off the illness, or an emotional or psychological trait may be detected that makes the patient susceptible to an illness. In both cases, the treatment can be targeted on the cause as well as alleviating the symptoms, leading to an ordered and permanent recovery.

So, having looked briefly at how and why healing works, let us look a little closer at the technique. Healing with energy consists of three main activities, though there are variations to suit individual cases. The first activity - the one most used by spiritualists - is to pass energy through the energy channels of the patient, usually by using physical contact - the *'laying on of hands'*. If everyone underwent this exercise once a week, with general healing energy being used, a lot of ailments would never manifest, as it works as a psychic antiseptic, removing the seeds of energy disorders, though its use against established illness is less effective.

The second activity is the application of specific energy to specific areas of the body/aura. This is done by a combination of using the hands to touch or come close to the area, and then visualising the complementary colour acting as a kind of sponge to 'soak up' the bad energies. This is the most effective method of removing symptoms, but will not cure them permanently unless the cause is removed.

The third action is to wash and infuse the whole aura with a colour or colours calculated to counteract the cause of the ailment, or any potential ailments detected. A combination of all three actions makes up a good basic healing technique.

Practical

The following list is of colours representing types of illness and cures. Generally speaking, the amount of colour indicates the stage of the illness (Some of the colour= tendency, a lot of the colour= illness present, colour is predominant = illness in full flight) and the darker the shade, the more serious the illness is.

Amethyst	Heart or stomach
Black	Mental illness. Yellow helps depression
Dark Grey	Emotional illness. White will help
Red	High blood pressure. Light green will help
White	Anaemia. Use brilliant white to cure
Orange	Too much = kidneys. Use purple to cure
Orange	Not enough = rheumatism, shyness

Yellow	Nervous energy
Dark Green	Depression.Used to cure high level of hysteria
Light Green	Cure for nerves
Blue	Good for general ailments causes calm
Turquoise	Mental recuperator
Light Blue	Emotional recuperator
Royal Blue	Physical recuperator
Indigo	Heart or stomach trouble. Can be used as an antiseptic, but keep clear of head - causes vertigo.

Obviously, in order to use this system, it is important to be able to detect the aura, and the following exercise will develop this ability if practised diligently.

If possible, work with a partner. If you do not have a partner to work with, use your right hand as a target. Firstly, meditate for a few minutes on the meaning of colour energy, and then look at your partner or hand. The background should be of a dark or neutral colour, preferably plain. Ideally a plain black or grey drape could be put up behind the target. The lighting should be dim, and candle-light is best.

Pick a point slightly above and to the right of your target - literally a few inches away, but on the background. Focus your eyes on this point, so that you see your target out of focus. As you look you will notice a smoky layer of greyish-blue around the target, perhaps half to one inch thick. This is the etheric layer of the aura, and the easiest part to see.

Examine it. The cleaner it looks, the healthier the patient is. As you examine the etheric layer, you will gradually become aware of areas of colour further away from the body as your vision becomes more attuned. This may take several sessions, but will eventually happen for everyone. If you do experience trouble at this stage, however, you will find in the appendix some other exercises that will help to train your eyes.

Once you are aware of the aura, practice looking at auras whenever possible. The more you use this ability, the easier it will become. When you can see the areas of colour well enough, start drawing them, and seeing what you can learn from the colours. You will learn more about the non-healing aspects of this in the lesson on auras.

Homework

Pick three different subjects, draw what you see of their aura, and write down a diagnosis of their condition, along with what you would do if you were treating them with colour healing.

Chapter 9

Candle Magic

Theory

The candle provides a living flame which has an astral counterpart, and some have called the flame "a rip in the fabric of reality". Flames are composed of pure energy, and have the property of fascination, focussing your attentions and energies onto a very small area, which aids concentration.

Flames respond readily to other energy forms, such as electromagnetic energy, and many people develop the ability to "control" candle flames, making them rise and fall, flutter and burn true, at will. Fire is the legendary gift of the gods, and has always had a religious/esoteric significance, and the ease with which wax is coloured has led to a simple but effective system of magic involving coloured candles coming into common use.

But what colours should you use? Most temples and lodges of the Mysteries make use of quarter candles at the cardinal points, and these are coloured to represent the element particular to that quarter, and candles on the altar, and those used for specific rites, are coloured in accordance with their purpose. The important point is that all of the candles in a rite must use the relevant colours from one system of colour correspondence - you can not expect Qabalistic quarter candles and Celtic working candle colours to mix happily.

Practical

This is only a brief and very basic introduction to candle magic - there will be much more later on in your training within a group or Lodge.

The first thing to do after selecting the colour of your candle is to dedicate it by annointing it with essential oil while concentrating on the use to which you will put it. You should ideally use an oil that corresponds to the purpose of the candle, but sandalwood is a good general-purpose oil. Place some of the oil in the palm of your left hand, and put the centre of the candle in it, clenching your hand around it. Draw the candle through your hand while twisting it, so that the oil is rubbed in a spiral from the centre of the candle to its top. Then repeat, going from the centre to the bottom. Hold the candle in both hands while pushing energy - visualised in the correct colour - into it until you feel you have done enough. Next place the candle in a holder somewhere safe - on your altar if the holder is a safe one, or away from combustible things - and allow it to burn down completely. If you wish, you can use one candle to represent the person the work is being done for - if other than yourself - and another candle for the energy.

To get rid of unwanted energy or negativity - even hostility towards someone - use a brown or black candle, and visualise pouring it all into the candle until you feel drained. Place the candle outside in the soil, and let it burn down, releasing the energy into the earth where it is neutralised. If you are in a block of flats, put some soil into a flowerpot and use that on a windowsill - do not use the peat from a growbag, as this is sterile and dead. Get some real soil from the local park, or a friend's garden.

Other variations include writing your intention on a strip of paper, and burning it in the candle, carving relevant symbols or words on the candle and burning it, or making up a blend of oils that is tuned to the required outcome and using that to anoint the candle. If it is necessary to put the candle out for any reason - and this includes quarter and altar candles after a circle has been closed down, snuff or pinch it out rather than blow it, as blowing can remove the charge of the candle in addition to splattering wax everywhere. A candle that needs to burn down can be snuffed and then relit later if the need arises - such as if you have nowhere safe to leave it so you have to watch over it, but need to go out for a while.

Homework

Try out the technique for some specific things, and record your results. Use a colour system that you are familiar with, or the basic list below.

Red	Love, change, energy
Orange	Spirituality, fortune
Yellow	Happiness, money
Green	Healing, family
Blue	Tranquillity, healing, psychic
Purple	Religion, leadership, mourning
White	Purification, children, general

Chapter 10

Elemental Magick

Theory

Elemental magick is based around the idea that everything in existence can be attributed to one of the classical elements, Air, Fire, Water, Earth, or Spirit. In fact, most things can be attributed to more than one element, but one will predominate. An example of this is a flower. Flowers in general come under the element of Air, due to their appearance in Spring, and the fact that plants draw nutrients from the air; but specific flowers may be placed elsewhere, or in several places according to what is being looked at.

Roses, for example, could be placed in the element of Water because they are associated with love, but a red rose could be placed in Fire due to its colour. This is not as contradictory as it seems, as the red rose is symbolic of passion, a fiery emotion, and spiritually represents transformation through growth (the bud becoming a flower). The important thing is to know the attributes of the element initially, and that is what we will concentrate on.

Air

This is the element of communication in all its forms, because all forms of communication travel through air, or are transmitted through things directly associated with Air. The spoken word, television, radio, and telepathy all convey information through the atmosphere. Blades are the *'weapons'* of Air, and the written word is written with the nib of a pen - a specialised blade - and is read using sight made possible by the existence of Light, which is represented by the element of Air (Air = Light, Fire = Life, Water = Love, Earth = Law). One of the most important forms of communication is the imparting of knowledge, so all learning is covered by the element of Air - and a mind keen to learn has always been called *'incisive';* indeed the word *'keen'* originally referred to the sharpness of a blade!

The last area of import covered by Air is medicine. As a science it is a form of communicated knowledge, and was originally the use of medicinal plants. Modern medicine has evolved a complex system of drugs - mostly derived from plants, though many are now synthesised - and surgery, with the scalpel of the surgeon being almost the archetypal *'weapon'* of this aspect of Air.

Fire

Fire is the element of transformation and energy. All substances and events that bring about change are included in this element, including war, inspiration, enlightenment. It is the element of that process of continuing transformation and energy, known as Life.

As fire is the great cleanser, the element of Fire has a healing aspect of purification, represented by antiseptics, and in their operation as preventors and protectors, the power represented by Fire can be seen. Fire can be a barrier, a transformer, a catalyst (heat), or can provide energy (generator, car engines, etc.), and so elemental Fire can do these things on a spiritual level.

Water

Still waters run deep' sums up this element. Water is the element of emotion, feelings, and psychic phenomena. If Air can be called the Realm of Thought, Fire the Realm of Action, and Earth the Realm of Stability, then Water is the Realm of Feeling (Spirit is, of course, the Realm of Becoming). Intuition, clairvoyance, love, and spiritual healing come under this element, and it finds its expression in poetry, fantasy, and day-dream.

Earth

The Firm Foundation upon which everything rests, is a good description of the element of Earth. It is the *'immovable object'* that traditionally meets the *'unstoppable force'* of Fire. It represents stability, certainty, and rigidity, and is the element of Law. As Earth, it is the closest spiritual aspect to the physical realm, and so represents material things - work, possessions, nature, death, and rebirth. It is seen as the unknown, the Initiator, the *'dark night of the soul'*.

In this element we meet the *'Dweller on the Threshold'*, for it is truly the doorway to the Underworld.

Weapons

Spirit

This element has been called many names, Ether, the Quintessence (literally, *'fifth thing'*), the Astral Planes, the Magickal Universe, but more than anything else, it is the source. The Realm of Becoming, it is the origin and the destiny of all things, the *'Abode of the Gods'* and the *'stuff of dreams'*. Very little can be said of this element, as its manifestation defies words, so your knowledge of it must be gained by experience.

Practical

The use of the elements in magickal ritual is quite straightforward. The appropriate element for the work is chosen, and that choice dictates the colour of candle, the godform/s, the incense, and the type of ritual, including the weapon used. Examples of these are given below.

Element	Weapon	Colour	Quarter	Godform	Rite
Air	Dagger	Blue	East	Thoth/ Osiris	Invoke
Fire	Wand	Red	South	Horus/ Sekhmet	Evoke
Water	Chalice	Green	West	Isis	Supplicate
Earth	Pantacle	Yellow	North	Anubis/ Nephthys	Meditate

Note: These are S.H.O.A.R allocations, and may differ from those of other systems.

To give a full example, let us look at a student who required a particular book for his studies. Books, of course, come under the element of Air as a form of communicating knowledge. Looking at the table, we can see that the student could call upon Osiris or Thoth, and as the matter concerns learning, he chooses Thoth, God of Learning and Science.

So, facing east, he lights blue altar candles, and after casting his circle in all *four* elements, he lights his air incense and invokes Thoth, asking for the book to be made available. A few days later, he receives a copy of the book as a late birthday present from his Aunt who is making one of her rare visits.

Within S.H.O.A.R there are set formulas for elemental workings, but with the above information, an ad lib invocation, and some bought incense, a good personal rite can be developed - with good visualisation, the key to all ritual.

Practical

Draw up four columns on a piece of paper, headed *air, fire, water,* and *earth,* and compile a list in each column of things that could be associated with that element - and be prepared to justify your choices. Choose a variety of physical objects, things you would find around the house, or in the street. Try some living things, plants and animals, and then start adding emotions and situations. See how many things you can add over the course of a week.

Homework

Continue the practical work, and then choose a problem or situation and write an elemental ritual to solve or help it.

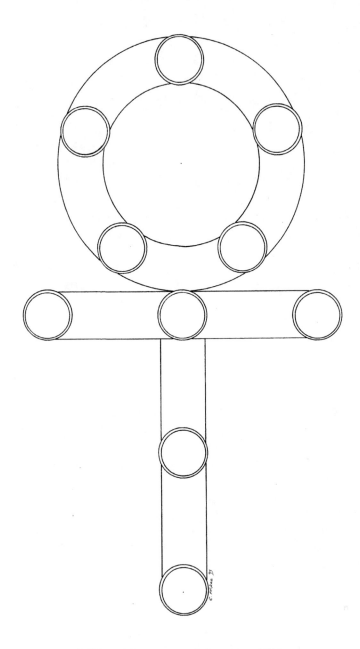

Ankh with speres of the tree of life

Chapter 11

The Ankh

Theory

The Ankh, known as the Egyptian Cross, and sometimes - if incorrectly - as the Tau Cross, is a symbol that conjures up Ancient Egypt in an instant. As a hieroglyph, it was used in two ways. Pronounced as *onkh* it meant *"key"*, and pronounced *"ankh"* it meant *"Life"*. From this it gained its commonly accepted interpretation of *"Key of Life"* or *"Tree of Life"*.

The Ankh consists of two parts, a Tau Cross *("T"*-shape) and a circle. The Tau consists of a central square with three arms, each containing three squares. This gives ten squares that are traditionally attributed to the spheres of the Qabalistic Tree of Life.

The circle, shown as a ring, consists of the centre, the inner boundary of the ring, and the outer boundary. To continue the Qabalistic correspondence, theses can be equated to the *void*, the *limitless*, and the *limitless light*. The Void, Ain in Hebrew, is in the Egyptian system the Nun, the primordial waters of chaos from which all sprang.

The Limitless, Ain Soph in Hebrew, is Atum, the Creator, self-formed, who united with the Nun to bring forth the manifest Universe. This is a condition where there is no limit by time and space, and there is infinite potential.

The Limitless Light - Ain Soph Aur - is the Manifest Universe at its moment of creation, and sees the Creator manifest within His creation as Ra. It is the Big Bang that started this universe with its concepts of time and space.

Another way of looking at these three *"veils"* at a more personal level is to see the void as Ra, the Limitless as Osiris, and the Limitless Light as Horus. Ra, as an aspect of the Creator is seen as distant and unapproachable. He sent Osiris as the First Manifestation of God among mortals, although he is not a complete manifestation until he undergoes his resurrection. He was the first mediator to teach humans the ways of the Divine.

Horus, son of Osiris, is seen as the incarnation of Ra, as the Solar Logos, a warrior placed in our world to combat the negative forces.

Tree of Life

It is possible to place the Tree of Life upon the entire Ankh, in a simplified form of the Ankh of Asar-Ra. Examples in the form of a Jewelled Ankh have been found in several tombs. In the full version of the Ankh of Aar-Ra, the arms are the wings of Isis, the circle is the Solar Disk encircled by the serpent, and the column is the Tet Column of Osiris.

Practical

The Ankh is an easily used key for meditation or astral travel to the Spiritual Land of Khem. For this reason, among others, it is seen as the Key to the Mysteries, and is often seen in the hands of deities symbolising the gift of Light, or Illumination. There is a secret to this, though. In some pictures, the deity is shown holding two Ankhs. This is to tell the reader that there is a hidden meaning to the accompanying text, in addition to the obvious one.

An iron ankh representing life and a stylised snake representing wisdom were used in the Ritual of the Opening of the Mouth, and by priests invoking a deity. In a simpler way, using the ankh in visualised form helps to charge talismans, amulets, and small devotional statues - within the circle environment, visualise a glowing golden ankh upon the object to be charged, and then *"see"* it being absorbed by the object.

The ankh is often used as a symbol of protection, particularly against *"anti-life"* influences. Wearing a charged ankh can help to seal your aura so that you do not get drained by *"psychic vampires"*, while many intuitive healers use the ankh for its life-giving symbolism. Some groups believe that the symbolism of the ankh holds the key to eternal life, and it does, in the spiritual sense. The symbol of the ankh is said to have been derived from the sandal straps of the priesthood, and here we see its use in charging and consecrating.

The priesthood of Ancient Egypt wore sandals of a particular design that had been consecrated in the Temple, so that they always walked on sacred ground. The sandals were woven from the papyrus reed, so that their footsteps symbolically walked the path laid out in the sacred writings - which also used papyrus as their basic material. If you meditate on all of the symbolism, especially the visual images associated with the ankh and its uses, you will find that gradually you come to understand just where the ankh belongs in the Mysteries, and how it truly is a key to the secrets of the Land of Khem.

Homework

Meditate on the Ankh, or do a pathworking using it as a gateway, and report your thoughts, findings, etc.

Chapter 12

Correspondences of Godforms

Theory

In most books on the deeper aspects of esoteric belief the *"Creator"* is seen as an infinite source of *"cosmic force"*, that brings creation into being through a series of controlled emanations of energy along clearly defined pathways. These pathways are identified by their frequency (the rate at which the energy wave vibrates) and modulation (the rate at which the actual energy vibrates when affected by other energy waves), giving them a characteristic *"vibration"*.

An example of this is the spectrum of visible colours. All light - indeed all energy - is the same, and the different colours are produced by the frequency of the light, long slow waves for reds, short fast ones for blues, etc. Frequency is merely a measurement of the rate of vibration of the energy wave. Modulation is what happens when there is more than one wave.

When two or more waves come together, they modulate either in unison, in harmony, or in disharmony. Sometimes two waves that are in harmony but are not synchronised can form a stable complex waveform that contains aspects

Horus, Osiris, Asar Ra, Ra, Anubis

of both. In audio terms this would result in a regular pulsed tone, and in the cosmic sense, it is displayed as a series of *"emanations"* of energy, such as the emanations said to be represented by the Qabalistic Tree of Life.

Depending on the tradition followed, there are said to be seven, nine, twelve, or forty-two rays emanating from the creator, each represented by a different colour.

All wave cycles vibrate in octaves which enable energies of a lower vibration than the main one to be *"in tune"* with it by being an exact number of octaves apart from it. Also, every form of energy is the same *"substance"* in varying rates of frequency, so the high vibrations of a cosmic ray can equate to a visible colour by the law of octaves, by matching its *"note"* in a different octave.

Each of these cosmic rays can be seen as representing - or being represented by - a particular deity, and all things that harmonise either directly or through the law of octaves with that ray can be said to correspond to that godform. This means, for example, that as the colour blue, healing and nature magic all have the same *"note"* as the Egyptian goddess Isis - though in different octaves - they equate or correspond to Her.

The effect of the complex waveform resulting from desynchronised harmonic waves is seen where a ray is represented by a paired deities, usually represented in the legends as husband and wife or twins.

A good example of this is the ray represented by Osiris and Isis, who are both partners and twins. Isis corresponds to blue and Osiris to green, and together they constitute the turquoise ray that is the core of the lesser mysteries of Ancient Egypt.

Hathor, Isis, Sekmet, Nepthys, Bast

Practical

The law of octaves is one of the deeper meanings of the phrase *"as above, so below"*. From this law we can find sounds, colours, smells, and other things that vibrate in harmony with the godform. By using images, colours, sounds, and smells, it is possible to *"tune-in"* to a particular godform, and that is the root of all ritual. Below is a list of deities with their colour, metal, and symbol. At a later date you can add the musical note, incense, and sound for each one.

GODFORM	COLOUR	METAL	SYMBOL
Osiris	Emerald Green	Gold	Crook & Flail
Isis	Egyptian Blue	Silver	Knot
Horus	Amber	"Fire Gold"	Eye
Bast	Turquoise	Copper	Sistrum
Anubis	Russet/Terracotta	Gold	Doorway
Hathor	Coral Pink	Pale Gold	Mirror
Ra	Deep Yellow	Deep Gold	Sun Disk
Ptah	Dark Blue	Bronze	Collar
Sekhmet	Crimson	Bright Gold	Ankh
Nephthys	Lilac	Silver	Basket
Thoth	Mauve	Old Gold	Scriber & Scroll
Asar-Ra	White	Gold	Ankh of Asar-Ra
Set	Blood Red	Copper	Sethian Beast

Please note that the colours are specific, and are as used within S.H.O.A.R. Meditation on these symbols and colours will give an insight into the natures of the deities.

Homework

Choose four godforms and meditate on them using the image of the symbol in metal on a background of the relevant colour. Record your results.

Chapter 13

Details of Godforms

Theory

Throughout history the human race has tried to personify the creator and/or aspects of the creator. The result is the various pantheons of deities found worldwide. The Egyptians were more open than most in that they acknowledged the fact that the *"gods"* were just aspects of the *"Hidden One"*.The association of a particular form of energy with a particular image over many thousands of years led to the powerful archetypes still present today as the gods and goddesses of the Nile Valley.

In order to make use of and work with these archetypes, it is necessary to be familiar with their form and function, and so below you will find a description of the main deities as used in S.H.O.A.R.

Osiris

Lord of the Underworld and Judge of the Dead. Osiris is pictured as a green-faced mummy wearing the white Atef crown and bearing the crook and flail. He is often seen seated on a throne at the top of a flight of seven steps. He is used in matters of law, agriculture, and initiation. He is the Midnight Sun.

Isis

Wife of Osiris and Queen of Heaven, she is the Mistress of Magick. Picture her as a beautiful lady in a blue dress and silver jewellery. On her head is a silver throne, or a crescent moon, and she is used in matters of magick, healing, and protection, especially of children.

Horus

The son of Osiris and Isis, Horus is a warrior clad in a golden breast-plate and yellow tunic, sometimes with a red cloak. His head is that of a hawk. Use him for protection, justice, and enlightenment, for he is the Solar Logos, a World Teacher.

Bast

The cat form of Hathor, she is goddess of music and can be playful. Her head is that of a cat, and her dress is turquoise. Call on her for artistic inspiration.

Anubis

This jackal-headed god is a walker-between-worlds, Guide of the initiate, and messenger of the gods. His jackal head is black - or, rarely, gold - and his robe is russet brown.

Hathor

The cow goddess is Mistress of Love and childbirth. Her dress is coral pink, and she appears as fully human with cow horns on her head, though sometimes with a full cow's head. Call on her for matters of love and happiness.

Ra

The Solar King. Ra has a hawk's head surmounted by a solar disk and his attire is of yellow and gold. Call on him for matters of leadership, life, and prosperity, the Sun at Noon.

Ptah

The Architect of the Universe, he wears a close-fitting skullcap headdress and a robe of deep blue. He is the Lord of Manifestation. Call on him to bring ideas to reality, and to lay firm foundations.

Sekhmet

The lioness-headed goddess is warrior, avenger, teacher, healer, and lover, all in one. Dressed in red, she wears a solar disk encircled by the cobra on her lioness head. Call on her in desperation, or to share love, and she will serve you well.

Nephthys

The dark side of Isis, she wears a lilac or pale green dress, and is Mistress of Divination. As Isis governs the creative aspects of nature - fertility, growth, etc. - so Nephthys governs the aspects of nature that break things down ready for re-use - decay, dissolution, etc.

Thoth

Scribe of the Gods, he is the origin of all knowledge and the inventor of writing. He wears a robe of amethyst, and his head is that of an ibis. He is always accompanied by an ape. Call on him in matters of learning, healing, and books.

Asar-Ra

The Uncreated Light, he is the twin souls of Osiris and Ra, which - according to legend - is all that will remain at the end of time. A falcon-headed god, dressed in white and with the double crown of Egypt, he also has the ram-skin of the creator draped over his shoulder. Call on him for protection from evil, and for guidance in the Inner Mysteries.

Set

Brother and slayer of Osiris, he is Lord of Storms and Desolation. Dressed in blood red, with the head of no creature on earth, call on him for revenge, murder and dark deeds, or to face the darkness within yourself.

Practical and homework

Visualise each godform within a circle, and see what you pick up from the image. Make sure to banish fully, and record your results. Refer to illustrations in this book, *The Book of the Veil*, or books such as the *Dictionary of Egyptian Gods and Goddesses* for reproductions of drawings of the deities, or visit the British Museum's Egyptian department.

Chapter 14

Use of Incense

Theory

There is probably not a single religion, faith, or Mystery that practices its rites free from the use of incense - in Christianity the swinging thurible is the hallmark of High Church ceremony, while in the eastern religions hardly a move is made without the appropriate incense being burnt.

Incense has always been used primarily as an offering to the gods, and it probably originated as the smoke from burnt offerings of animal sacrifices, rare herbs, and so on. Psychically aware priests would have noticed the different subtle vibrations released as the offerings smouldered, and careful examination and experimentation would have shown that these vibrations could be used to classify various substances for particular uses. As time went by, mixtures were developed that contained harmonic ingredients that augmented and multiplied in effect, and as knowledge grew, the incenses became more complex and specific, and the blending of them became an occult art in its own right.

There are three basic reasons for burning incense during ritual, and the most basic is *"to create atmosphere"*.

Everyone has had the experience of a lost memory being triggered by a smell, both pleasant and otherwise, and psychologists will vouch for the power of such effects. From the magical point of view, this can be useful in two ways: the association of certain scents with specific types of ritual helps to condition the student to enter the correct frame of mind right from the beginning of the rite; and the use of traditional incenses may trigger memories/abilities from past lives.

The next reason is that the vibrations of the incense help *"tune"* the energy used in the rite, and that is why it is important to use an appropriate incense - indeed the proper use of an expertly mixed incense is a powerful ritual in its own right. Not only do the vibrations *"direct"* the energy, but they can amplify it too.

Lastly, incense can be used as a basis for materialisation. Although this is rarely necessary, it can be useful and a billowing cloud of magically charged smoke is an effective aid.

Many people use incense because they like it, or because it is the *"done thing"*, without really understanding how or why it should be used. During your training within a working group you will learn how to make incense and use it effectively.

Practical

The most important thing to learn about incense is how to burn it properly. The verb *"burn"* is actually not very accurate, as the actual process is to smoulder the incense. Stick and cone incense is lit, and then allowed to go out, so that it has a glowing tip like a cigarette, but loose ritual incense must be smouldered on a charcoal block, and this is the tricky part.

The first requirement is to use a proper container. Any heat-proof bowl will do, though most prefer a proper censor. At first, use one with a stable base rather than a chain thurible, as the burning and swinging are separate arts. The bowl or censor should be half-filled with fine silver sand or salt - this helps to insulate the container, and also places the charcoal block where the air gets to it best. Hold the charcoal block in a candle flame, using a largish pair of tweezers, and wait for the sparkler effect to finish.

The candle flame may blow out during this, so be prepared to relight it. When the sparkling has stopped, remove the block from the flame and blow on it gently. It should glow red in places, and as you blow it will eventually all glow red. Place it in the bowl, hollow side up, and wait until the surface has turned white/grey with a thin film of ash (a few minutes), then place a pinch or two of incense on the block, and as it smoulders, the aroma is released.

Although the recipes for different incenses are likely to have similarities from group to group - due to the universal nature of the correspondence of ingredients - there will be differences, so it is not practical to provide a comprehensive *"cookbook"* of recipes (though if you want such a book, there are several available, such as *Wylund's Book of Incense*, and *Scott Cunningham's Incenses, Oils and Brews*). However, for the student who does not have the fortune of belonging to a group, here are some Egyptian incense recipes that are used within S.H.O.A.R.

General Egyptian Incense

Camphor oil	2 drops
Laurel or bay leaves	2 parts
Salt	1 part
White resin or Lavender	4 parts
Dragon's Blood	1/4 part
Sandalwood oil	6 drops
Myrrh	4 parts

Astarte

Sandalwood
Rose
Orange oil
Jasmine

Cleopatra

Pine Bark
Sandalwood
Orris root
Patchouli
Myrrh
Frankincense
Wood base

Kyphi

Resin (benzoin)
Galangal root
Juniper berries
Aromatic Rush

Asphaltus
Mastic
Grapes
Honey
Wine
Myrrh

Isis

Myrrh
Vetavert
Frankincense
Orange rind
Civit
Styrax
Myrtle

Osiris

Lavender
Lemon
Violet
Orris root
Cardomon

Egyptian Temple

Myrrh Balm of Gilead
Frankincense
Orange peel
Lotus
Costus (sweet flag)

Thoth

Lavender
Mastic
Cinnamon

Sekhmet

Verbena or Vetavert
Galangal root
Peppermint
Rue
Cinnamon

Anubis

Cinnamon
Cedar oil
Orris oil
Myrrh

Where no amounts are given, it is traditional to use equal amounts of each ingredient, but the cost of some ingredients - and the smell of others - makes the blending of an incense a very personal matter. Start by familiarising yourself with the individual smells, and any ingredients you do not like the smell of can be used in very small quantities. But be prepared to experiment, because there are some foul-smelling substances - such as asafoetida - that smell awful by themselves but in combination with other ingredients lose their own smell and enhance the smell of the other components.

When mixing the ingredients, first grind them as finely as is practical. The finer the incense, the more smoke and scent it will release, and the more uniform the result will be. Obviously, some ingredients are difficult to grind, and sometimes you might prefer the texture and changing scent of a coarser incense, but once again this is down to personal judgement.

Mix the dry ingredients first, then add the liquids - enough to dampen the rest, but not to make a paste. Essential oils should be used by the drop, and yes, you can substitute oils for dry ingredients, but make sure that the oils are pure and not synthetic - synthetic oil smells like burning plastic when used in an incense, and does not carry the right vibrations.

If you can not get a particular ingredient, it is possible to use a substitute, or if the incense has a lot of ingredients, miss it out - as a last resort. Health food and herbalist suppliers will be able to sell you many if not all of the ingredients, but a specifically occult supplier, such as Occultique in Kettering Road, Northampton (Tel. 01604 27027) will be able to advise you on substitutions, as well as other recipes.

Homework

Obtain a small selection of made-up incenses and individual ingredients, and burn them one at a time. See what impressions you pick up, and note their smell and the effects on you and the room you are in. Comment on possible uses.

Chapter 15

Meditation

Theory

Perhaps the one spiritual exercise common to every faith, religion, and system, meditation is simultaneously over and under estimated in its usefulness by 90% of practitioners.

As it is basically a method of altering consciousness, and promotes a sense of well-being, many see it as no more than a form of relaxation. Others see its mind-altering properties as a solution to all the problems in the world.

The average magician sees meditation as a necessary part of training to develop the concentration and focus required in ritual, but of no real value as a magical tool, but it is a fact that its use in combination with other techniques augments the effectiveness of those techniques to an amazing degree.

The main aim of meditation is to turn the consciousness inward to seek the sacred space within. Most groups follow the eastern technique of attempting to empty the mind of all conscious thought, but this is only one way of achieving a result, and of little value to the student magician due to the timescale involved, although gaining this state of

Samadhi (unity with the void) is used at more advanced levels.

The method used in S.H.O.A.R. is a more dynamic one. Rather than emptying the mind, it is allowed to flow in a direction dictated by the conditions present - atmosphere, prior work, chanting, etc. In fact, just sitting quietly thinking about a topic and seeing where it takes you is a valid starting point, and one that can have profound results. The main requirements for successful meditation are freedom from distractions and the ability to focus on a given topic, which develops with practice.

But what happens when you meditate? Basically, the mind reduces its activity as far as conscious processes are concerned, and the subconscious activity increases and impinges on the subject's awareness. In more technical terms, the brain produces fewer beta waves and more alpha waves. These alpha waves are of a higher vibration than normal thought, increasing the possibility of interaction from higher aspects of the self.

Obviously this alpha state is very useful when performing rituals, as invocation, mediation, even the charging of a talisman all involve contacting higher entities through the higher self. But not all methods of achieving this state are of practical use in this way.

For example, many of the complicated positions, or asanas, of Yoga provide a relatively quick and easy entrance to the state, but take months to master comfortably and can not be moved out of without returning to normal consciousness.

By far the most practical aid to the meditative state is chanting, as it requires no machinery or special substances, takes minutes rather than months to learn, and can be stopped without significantly affecting the altered state of mind. Resuming the chant at the end of the meditation can be used to aid return to normal consciousness in a controlled manner.

For general meditation, any chant can be used; your own name, a passage from a book, or the famous *"Om mani padne hum"* of the Tibetan Bhuddists. In fact, the more meaningless the phrase or mantra is to you, the more effectively it will work. But for magical meditation, something more specific is required.

In every system there is a collection of phonic groups that make up the *"words of power"* of that system, each with its own particular meaning. These words of power may be used as mantras in specific situations, such as the NA-EN-TA in Enochian magick, which is used to summon the power of the element of Earth.

In addition, many systems also link a musical note to each syllable. Providing the system has the correct notation, the note for a particular syllable will be a harmonic vibration of the energy represented by that syllable, thus reinforcing the effect of the mantra both as an alpha-state inducer and as a focus for the purpose of the meditation. An example of this from ancient Egypt is the use of a secret Temple Name for the deity, known only to the priests of that temple, which could be chanted by the Priests as the High Priest invoked the deity in the sanctuary.

Practical

If you should begin to attend S.H.O.A.R rituals, you will find that there is a group meditation in every rite, and it is important that you know the mechanics of it. There are three important phases, the position, the chant, and the visualisation.

Position

This is basically the position you see demonstrated in the statues of seated deities from Egypt. With the back upright and feet together, flat on the floor, place your hands palm down on your thighs, and face straight ahead, but looking slightly upward. With your eyes closed, you are in the meditative position.

Chant

This is a simple chant, "RA-MA". Each syllable is chanted on its own note, the RA being lower than the MA. The syllable RA is the Divine Father, representing the masculine creative principle (the male orgasm is accompanied by vocalisations of RA or very similar sounds - where inhibitions do not interfere - even if they are not audible).

The syllable MA is the Divine Mother, representing the feminine creative principle (once again, this is vocalised during female orgasm). Together they represent the harmony and balance of the sexual polarities, enabling a greater degree of union with the Divine Will than would otherwise occur.

The chant is begun by the Celebrant, who sets the notes, and it is taken up by everyone else. After a short time, the Celebrant stops, and everyone else continues until they feel the need to stop.

At the end, the Celebrant chants three times to bring everyone back. The phrase is chanted to a strict measure of 4-4-8: ie., RA for four beats, MA for four beats, silence for eight beats. As you will come to realise, the silence is as important as the sounds.

Visualisation

If there is a specific visualisation, the Celebrant will describe it, but usually the Lodge members concentrate initially on the Temple visualisations. If something of significance intrudes, however, they will follow the new visualisation.

Homework

Experiment using your name as a mantra, and record your results.

Chapter 16

Principles of the Path of Light

Order and Chaos

The forces of Order are those in favour of life, working through the evolutionary process. They are the Gods of Light, angels, Lords of Life, and so on. Sekhmet is a Warrior of Order. The goal of the evolutionary path is unity with Divinity.

The forces of Chaos are those forces that are anti-life, working through the process of devolution. They are seen as devils, demons (in the Christian sense), and Chaotic Beings. Set is a Warrior of Chaos who, although he ultimately serves the Light, is a hater of Life and Order. He creates changes that can promote growth but unchecked will lead to destruction.

Chaotic humans (*"Black magicians"*) do not in their ideal get reabsorbed into the Group Soul after death; and therefore cannot be reborn as part of the cycle of life. If they wish to reincarnate they have to use their own power, and as they cannot draw on cosmic energy due to their opposition to it, they draw on the power of their followers, using psychic vampirism to bleed off the energy of those around them.

When they evoke, the circle they use allows a chaos entity to exist temporarily in this realm, much as a goldfish may reside in a living room as long as it is in its bowl. Most do not realise this, thinking that the circle is merely for their own protection. They strike bargains with these entities in order to reduce risk to themselves and to gain temporary power.

The chaotic entities may be considered to be intruders from another dimension, a universe that is limited - unlike ours - and in which the dominant force is anti-life. Their ultimate goal is to destroy life in our universe so that they can colonise it. This may sound a bit *"science fiction"*, but chaotic entities are a real force that you will no doubt encounter during your magickal career, as all genuine magickal events attract them, though they cannot penetrate the protection of the Lords of Light unless invited.

Please note that so-called Chaos Magick is not necessarily Chaotic Magick - much of it is based on pre-dynastic Egyptian Shamanism - but some definitely is anti-life, just as there are anti-life Egyptian Magicians, and in all other systems there are those known as the *"Black Brethren"*.

You may wonder why this information is being included. The answer is that by being aware of the *"enemy"* we can avoid falling into their trap. The information will help you in two ways. Firstly, it will enable you to avoid becoming *"lured to the dark side"* as you will be aware of the pitfalls of anti-evolutionary forces.

The chaotic magician bets their very existence on being able to become sufficiently adept in one lifetime that they can force a reincarnation for themselves, or avoid physical death altogether. This is a huge gamble, and as time passes becomes a greater and greater part of the chaotic magician's life, as they work *"against the clock"* to prevent their own destruction.

The second way that the information will help you is in choosing whether to join a group when you find one. A group set up to provide its leaders with energy from the lesser members is fairly easy to spot when you know what to look for, so you can avoid becoming involved with one.

The first thing you will notice is that such a group has leaders who are practically worshipped by their followers, but who seldom have direct contact with them. We are, of course, talking about individual groups here, not large organisations, who also have this trait, but for different and more acceptable reasons. The leader of such a chaotic group will be too busy working towards his or her survival to waste time training the recruits in the modicum of occult lore needed to make them efficient energy providers - this will be delegated to others. A true teacher of the Mysteries, conversely, will always be accessible to the group at all levels, especially as these groups tend to be small, rarely being larger than about eight members.

This leads to the second identifying fact. Chaotic groups tend to be larger, as recruits are attracted to the charismatic leadership, and few are turned away. A true teacher of the Mysteries is usually difficult to discover, and will turn away far more potential recruits than they will accept. Of course, those who are accepted will learn a lot, and will go on learning for the rest of their time in the group. Chaotic recruits, on the other hand, will only learn enough to direct their energies at the leaders, and after a month or so only those with potential to fill vacancies in the hierarchy will continue to learn. Meanwhile, they will be kept occupied with flashy rituals, sexual indulgences, drugs, and anything else that will keep them amused while the leaders get on with their survival rites. In the end many become disillusioned, and move on. Followers of a true teacher tend to stay with them for years unless other factors, such as group politics interfere.

Generally speaking, these groups do not usually cause any real or lasting harm to their followers. The biggest harm is in delaying the spiritual evolution of those involved. They may even serve a useful purpose, attracting those on the fringe of the Mysteries, the sensation seekers, the disturbed, and the would-be power-mongers. While they may use soft drugs and promiscuity as a lure, criminal activities beyond this are extremely rare, as the leaders need to avoid the interference of the authorities.

Chapter 17

Protection

Theory

It is important to differentiate psychic attack from other things that are often mistaken for such an attack. The various symptoms of an attack can have psychological, physiological, or psychic causes. If you enclose the subject - or yourself if you are the one under attack - in a circle with the intent of purification and the symptoms stop, then the cause is either psychic or psychological. If they do not stop, then consult a healer or medic.

The Sphere of Light exercise is particularly good at screening attacks - and remember that an attack can be from within yourself as easily as from another person - as it purifies the body and aura, thus eliminating any psychic residue.

A psychic attack will not usually return when the circle is removed, but a psychological one probably will. If it does, you can either attempt to work on it yourself through meditation, ask the opinion of another person, or seek professional help if necessary.

If you have established that the attack is a genuine psychic one, what do you do next? Firstly you must negate the effects - the symptoms:

Draining

This is the commonest symptom of attack, and is caused by psychic vampirism. Remember that this can be done unconsciously, and that the *"attacker"* may not even know what they are doing. There will be a psychic link between yourself and the attacker, so do the following.

> Place your knees and feet together with your hands clasped over your solar plexus. You may either sit or stand for this. Visualise the link as a muddy band attached to your body and leading away. See yourself holding a sword in one hand and a flaming torch in the other, cut the bond with the sword and cauterise the end with the flame. Not only does this end the draining of energy, but makes the *"attacker"* unlikely to try again.

If you are the victim of energy draining, try not to feel badly toward the *"attacker"*, as few people have the knowledge to do this deliberately.

Other symptoms

If you are experiencing other types of attack, and are certain that a particular person is responsible, perform the Sphere of Light and visualise the outside surface as mirrored.

Traditionally this reflects what they are sending back to them seven-fold. If you know who it is and have a picture or photograph of them, put it facing a mirror, which will have the effect of making them *"see"* what they are doing.

Psychic attack from astral entities

Psychic *"pests"* are attracted by most forms of psychic work in the same way that mosquitoes are attracted to sweat. Cats are good at catching and dispersing them, and they are easily banished by casting a circle or drawing a banishing Earth pentagram at them.

Malevolent astral entities can be encountered in three ways. Firstly, a group could conjure one and set it on you - very unlikely. Secondly, you could accidentally desecrate a sacred place, in which case you will encounter its guardian - if you are sensible, you will only encounter them as benign beings. Finally, you can attract or conjure them yourself by mistake or as the result of ignorance.

If any of these happen, get yourself into a position of protection;ie. , in a circle or sphere of light, with your feet together and hands clasped over your solar plexus. If you are competent at invocations and can recognise the entity or its nature - or can deduce the likely type of entity - invoke a powerful deity who will be able to get rid of it. In extremis, invoke Thoth or Asar-Ra or Sekhmet. You could use an exorcism, such as that of the catholic church, if you know one.

One note: in the unlikely event that someone has sent the Angel of Death against you, it is traditionally said that he must take a life, and will take the sender's if necessary. But anyone with enough skill and *"power"* to do this would not waste their time with you unless you have caused them serious problems, and most adepts would never do anything to incur the negative karma this act would place on them.

If you are in your circle, but are unable to get rid of the entity, do not forget that the circle will move with you if you will it to - particularly the Sphere of Light. Get to someone who can help you, or onto sacred ground - the old superstition is true about evil spirits not being able to walk on sacred ground, but it must be *real* sacred ground. In many cases, particularly where a guardian is involved, just moving out of the area will do the trick, but regardless, make sure that someone comes back to *"clean up"* afterward!

Prevention

Stay out of trouble, and you will not invite or invoke psychic attack. This means being honest and avoiding underhand activities - two things you should be observing as a student of the Mysteries anyway. Learn your basic training - the Sphere of Light can be developed as a reflex action, so you would automatically repel attacks without even being aware of most.

If you think an attack is likely, get your defences up first - use a stronger circle, be ready for trouble, and above all, ensure that your mental, physical, and spiritual selves are as balanced - both elementally and with each other - as they can be. Lastly, don't allow negative feelings or thoughts build up, but deal with them. Then *you* won't be inadvertently responsible for a psychic attack on another person.

Practical

This is how a student described a psychic attack that was part of a training workshop:

"Your heart skips beats, your balance goes, and there is a coldness inside. It feels as if someone is flicking at your eyes. "

The technique that had been used on her was a simple one. The tutor visualised a multi-coloured mass of colour with spikes swirling anticlockwise, and pushed it at her. An interesting note is that such a swirl appears to turn anticlockwise whichever direction it is observed from.

The way to neutralise this *"attack"* is to visualise another mass, swirling clockwise and push it at the negative swirl. If the attack was perceived as one colour, the complimentary colour could be used. If the defence is charged with energy drawn from the earth or sky, it will result in a quick disconnection from the *"attacker"*.

Homework

Practice the Sphere of Light as a daily routine, If you have a partner, practice defending against the "swirl" type of attack using different methods. If you do not have a partner, it will be difficult to practise using the swirl, but you can - if your visualisation ability is good - set an anticlockwise swirl against yourself and neutralise it. If you do this, though, use pale colours so that the effect is not damaging in any way if you fail to stop it.

Chapter 18

Unity With Divinity

Theory

In his novel *"Stranger in a Strange Land"*, Robert Heinlein raised an idea that led to him being accused of blasphemy by the church, and made the book one of the most controversial of its time. It is now a classic.

The idea he raised? That God is in us and we are all, because of that, God incarnate. The book explores the ramifications of the statement *"I am god, you are god"* through the actions of the hero, Michael Valentine Smith, who performs miracles simply because he had never ever been told that anything was impossible; but this idea was not a new one.

The concept of the *"God Within"* has always been a part of the Mysteries. Indeed, the true aim of the magician, his Great Work, is neither more nor less than linking the divinity within to the waking consciousness. In the days of the Golden Dawn and Aleister Crowley it was called *"attaining the knowledge and conversation of one's Holy Guardian Angel"*, but today we talk of "tuning-in" to the Higher Self.

The reasoning behind the assumption that we all possess this Higher Self, this *"divine spark"*, is quite simple. If the universe is a series of emanations of energy by the Creator, then the universe IS the Creator. That makes us a part of Him/Her/It, and what we are part of is also part of us.

Eastern mystics take this literally, and turn inwards to find divinity through contemplation, turning away from the illusion of the material world.

The western magician, however, recognises that the universe is God made manifest, and uses his environment as a tool to look past the illusion and *"gaze on the face of God"* - and when they get there, the face they see is their own.

But why look for this link with divinity? The answer lies at the core of the secret teachings of all Mysteries, and is a simple one - unity with divinity is the requirement for completing the cycle of incarnation.

At its most basic, the momentary unity with the Higher Self that takes place during a perfect ritual or meditation is a moment of enlightenment where guidance is given. It happens to everyone at odd moments in their life when the conditions are right, and is almost never expected.

Moving a stage further, the magician learns to induce the moment of unity by providing the right conditions: training in ritual sets the scene, practice and further training of a non-ritual nature develops the concentration and ability to focus until the magician can be fairly confident, if not totally certain, that the moment of unity will come at the climax of the work. From there it is a matter of further practice and training to turn the moment into a longer event, until eventually the adept is able to enter the state for as long as is needed. Finally the state becomes permanent, and the Master either moves on to further cycles of existence, or chooses to remain as a teacher.

Practical

How does one practice unity with the Higher Self? First, you must look at the past, and identify events that might have been such moments: times of great stress, when the solution *"popped in"* from nowhere; times of sorrow or depression, where an inner voice brought peace; any time when an unexplained phenomenon either solved or enabled you to solve a problem. Think about it: meditate on it: write them down. Then look at the circumstances. Usually you have tried everything else, there is no hope, yet you dare to hope for a miracle. You open yourself up - for you have nothing to lose - and, consciously or unconsciously, you call for help.

Christians use a phrase, *"God helps those who help themselves"*, and this applies regardless of the deity concerned. Magick is not the easy way out. If you attempt to achieve something by magick that you could have done without it, success will only come when you have expended at least as much effort as if you had done it by normal means.

If success by any other means is impossible, and *you have tried*, provided that your need is great enough and you work to your training, you will achieve results with magick, often accompanied by a brief moment of unity with divinity. Of course, much of your work will be aimed purely at gaining that moment of unity rather than physical benefit.

The Egyptians looked on the Higher Self as the *"Man made God"*, and devised ways of temporarily becoming the perfect Self in order to work miracles - assuming the Body of Light in its true sense. Later training will make you aware of these techniques, but for now practice ways of contacting that self, however briefly. Try the following exercises.

1.   Meditate on a point of light deep in your heart, of a warm golden colour. Record your feelings/impressions.

2.   Visualise yourself rising up a shaft of light toward its source. Try and go as high as you can, and at that point remain for as long as possible before sinking back down. Record impressions/feelings/images.

3.   Meditate using your name as a mantra, while in the Sphere of Light. Record your results.

Homework

Try each of the exercises, at least twice, recording your results. How does repetition affect your results?

Chapter 19

Spiritual Evolution

Theory

In the religion of Ancient Egypt, the leading figure is Horus, son of Isis and Osiris. These three were placed on the three sides of a triangle - that symbol so favoured by the Egyptians. But this was not just an ordinary triangle, but a right-angled one, with a vertical of three units representing Osiris, a horizontal of four units representing Isis, and a hypotenuse of five units representing Horus. This triangle, whose mathematics was revealed by Pythagorus, an initiate of the Egyptian Mysteries, can be examined in detail to produce a wealth of information concerning among other things, spiritual evolution. For the purposes of this lesson we will not restrict ourselves to Egypt, but examine correlations that are universal.

In the Egyptian language Horus is known as Khoor, which is represented by two hieroglyphs corresponding to Chi and Rho in the Greek alphabet, Kaph and Resh in the Hebrew, and C and R in our alphabet. Chi and Rho are the letters used to form the monogram of Christ in the Catholic Church, and C. R. is the only appellation given for the founder of the Rosicrucian Order.

Masonic legend has it that when Pythagoras discovered the secret of the triangle, he shouted *"Eureka!"*, which has a numerical value of 534, itself expressing the value of the sides of the triangle. Hermetic philosophers once summarised the Great Work as *"not only one and three, but withal four and five, and this truth is essential."* There are only two symbols corresponding exactly to this description, the Pythagorean triangle, and the Great Pyramid, both of Egyptian origin - the pyramid is a single solid, with three-sided faces (3), a square base (4), and five corners. The Great Work is declared to be an operation of the Sun and the Moon, and the triangle represents Horus (Sun), Isis (Moon), and Osiris (Can be attributed to either or both).

From alchemy, we learn that the Great Work depends on three principles, Mercury, Sulphur, and Salt, with Mercury being first as it is the principle by which the work of the Sun and Moon is done. As Sulphur is the second principle, representing change, and salt represents fixation, we have an order for them, and so they are placed on the Osiris line in that order.

The four units of the Isis line can be assigned to the four elements, Fire, Water, Air, and Earth. Finally, to the hypotenuse is assigned the ascending kingdoms of manifestation. Nearest the base, and next to Earth is the mineral kingdom, followed by the vegetable, animal, and human kingdoms. The final unit is the divine, following the Qabalistic saying, *"First the stone, then the plant, then the animal, then the man, and after man - God."* Horus the Son is the cosmic Life Spirit ascending this evolutionary ladder of form, one kingdom emerging from another.

But the story does not end there. The triangle has three angles. The first is ninety degrees, formed by the junction of the Isis and Osiris lines, and 90 is the value of the Hebrew word MIM, water, representing the generative potency of the union of the Father and Mother, giving birth to the Son.

The angle formed by the Isis and Horus lines is 37 degrees. This number is of immense importance in Christian secret doctrine, there being a book, *'Apostolic Gnosis'* which gives a whole series of names and titles of Christ which are numerically 37 or a multiple of 37. In Hebrew, 37 is the value of the name Abel, the Son of Adam murdered by Cain, accepted by theologists of all denominations as a prototype of Christ, and is an expression of the changeful nature of manifested existence.

When the Old Testament was translated into Greek, the word used for the Ark of both Noah and Moses was *he thibe,* with a value of 37, which is a transliteration of the Hebrew ThBH (Taybaw), which is 37 x 11, or 407, which symbolises *he kleronomia, 'The Inheritance'.* A number specifically associated with the Ark in the Jewish religion is the number eight, as eight humans were saved, and this is the number corresponding to the current of the mysteries which includes Hermetics, Rosicrucianism, and S. H.O. A.R.

Throughout the Old Testament, those against God are linked to the number thirteen, while those on God's side are linked to the number eight (An interesting thought considering the most prominent New Testament Group of thirteen, Christ and the disciples!). But scholars have missed the fact that thirteen is also a symbol of divinity, as most of the principle names of God in the Scriptures are multiples of thirteen, and two words much used in the Hebrew scriptures which are of value 13 are the words for unity and love. Added together, these two words give 26, the value of the name Jehovah. 2 and 6 add to make eight.

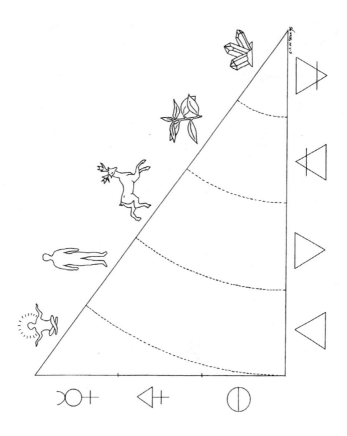

The Pythagorean Triangle

But what has this to do with the triangle? Well, the definition of the Great Work given by alchemy was that it was 1, 3, 4, and 5, which add up to thirteen. The triangle is one figure containing 3, 4, and 5 also, so can signify the number 13.

The hypotenuse is a very special line. Its first segment is attributed to the vegetable kingdom. An arc drawn down from the upper end of this segment meets with the Isis line at the end of the earth segment, and the link here is obvious. The second segment is the vegetable kingdom, and an arc drawn from the end of it meets the end of the air segment of Isis. A major characteristic of plants is their use of the earth and the air for nourishment. The animal kingdom segment produces an arc that meets the Water section of Isis, and the principle constituent of animal bodies is water - blood has been described as modified sea-water, and science tells us that animal life had its beginnings in the sea.

The segment for Man shows several things. As in all the segments, the 37 degree angle with the base line is implied, showing that man is evolved from the kingdoms but still has the same fundamental relationship to nature. An arc drawn here meets the end of the Fire section, and the point where the base and the perpendicular meet - man is the only creature who knows how to master fire, and with the ability to understand the secret of generation represented by the union of Osiris and Isis.

This does not mean that all men can do this, but that those who penetrate the heart of the Mystery may discover how to carry themselves beyond the limits of Homo Sapiens into the fifth kingdom, by fulfilling the Great Work. Those who follow the Way of Liberation to its end reach the point that is the beginning of the Osiris line. The goal of the Son is union with the Father and release from the *'Dominion'* of the Elements, an arc drawn from this point meets no obstacles, and forms a complete circle, symbol of eternity, and of Divinity.

Having a radius of 5, this circle has a diameter of 10. Its circumference is 31. 42, which the ancients took to be 32. Ten is the number of spheres on the Tree of Life, and upon it are 22 paths, giving a total of 32. To arrive at the completion of the Great Work is to pass out of the limitations of Time into the freedom of Eternity.

Throughout the ascent of the Horus Line, the relation between Horus and Isis, Developing Form and Nature, is expressed by the 37 degree angle. This relation does not change when the Work is completed, but something is added. The Son is conjoined with the Father, at the point symbolised in the Tree of Life by Kether, the Crown. The angle at this point is 53 degrees.

From the very beginning at the Isis line, the Horus line is always pointing directly at this final point, and so the angle of 53 degrees is implied throughout evolution - it is always the goal. 53 is the value of the Hebrew word ABN, Ehben, which means stone. The first two letters spell AB, which means Father, and the last two BN, which means Son. As a Qabalistic Alchemist might say, in the stone (ABN) the powers of the Father (AB) and the Son (BN) are conjoined.

The power of the Qabalistic *'Father'* is Chockmah, Wisdom, which is called AB by Qabalists, and its special force, its secret power, is Life-Force.

BN is the special name given by Qabalists to the sphere of Tiphareth, and represents manifestation in the World of Action, the physical plane. Thus it can be seen that the union of the Son and the Father enables the Life-Force of the Divine to manifest upon the physical plane.

Those trained in the magickal arts attain a temporary union during invocation, but those rare entities who fulfil their goal of becoming *more than human* are free to depart the cycle of reincarnation. There is much argument over whether this entails leaving the physical realm, or may include physical immortality - an option certainly implied by esoteric Christian teaching, but what is certain is that the great Masters of history, Enoch, Imhotep, Bhudda, Christ, Mohammed, and Thoth, were all supreme Masters who attained their goal and spent a while teaching in this world before proceeding to the next.

Practical

As your entire life is a practical exercise along the lines given, there is no exercises that can be given, although meditation and discussion on the subjects raised will be helpful to you.

Homework

Pick a symbol of importance to yourself, and analyse it as deeply as you can with reference to yourself. Draw on any reference material or tradition you wish.

Chapter 20

Elements Of Ritual

Theory

What is a ritual? Any task that you carry out in a *"certain way"* is a ritual. For example, the way you get into and start your car, the way you get dressed, these are all rituals within your daily life.

Obviously, though, magical ritual needs further definition. Basically, ritual is the act of focussing your will upon the desired outcome - all else is detail. A great mystic chanting for world peace, or a master magician performing evocations for the same end, are both undertaking ritual activities, albeit at opposite extremes of the scale.

For the purposes of your present training, we will be concentrating on what is conventionally considered to be ritual - the casting of a circle, wearing robes, etc. Ritual is a very important part of magical work, but not as important as you might think - a person who undertakes the training and does no ritual will still be a better human being, and more spiritually advanced, but someone who attempts to practice the rituals without the training will always fail, and his/her failure will discourage further study.

Looking at the definition again, the key word is *"focus"*. This is a form of single-pointed concentration which enables the magician to break through the limitations imposed by upbringing and social conditioning.

A magical rite actually starts long before it is actually performed. The moment you decide to do a ritual, you enter the first stage, preparation. The first thing to do is to establish the aim of the rite, which should be stated in a single sentence that is not too long. For this example we will use a fairly mundane aim: getting a job. At this point we must stress that you must make non-magical effort towards mundane goals as well as ritual - it is no use working to win the lottery if you do not buy a ticket in the first place!

Having established your aim, you must decide what form to use. Employment comes under material prosperity, while getting a job involves someone making a decision. In Egypt, Ra governs prosperity while Maat, his consort, symbolises justice. By using Ra and Maat we combine the two aspects and also automatically work in harmony with our destiny, for Maat is the balance on the Scales of Karma - we will get the job that is meant for us.

We then construct a ritual using elements that correspond to Ra and Maat - the appropriate colours, numbers, incense, invocations, music, etc. Then we are ready to start.

The opening of the ritual should be a declaration of intent to the deities involved, followed by casting the circle. Naturally the circle should harmonise with the purpose and the deities - you would not cast a Tibetan circle to call on Egyptian deities.

Once the circle is up there is a pure and sacred space in which to invite the deities, and the Watchtowers are summoned to guard and assist in the rite. Without the circle to contain it, the energy would not build up to the necessary level for a successful invocation.

The invocation should consist of three sections: firstly the deity should be hailed and asked to come; then the deity should be spoken to as if present; finally the magician speaks *as* the deity, assuming the relative postures if appropriate.

The aim is then stated as an accomplished fact, and is visualised as an accomplished thing. This visualisation is then earthed, perhaps in a talisman, or in a chalice of wine to be drunk, or a simple stamp of the foot. The deity is allowed to depart, and the circle is closed down.

For some purposes the ritual needs to be repeated, usually three or seven times, and if this is, or appears to be, the case, it must be done exactly the same each time.

Practical

We will now look at a popular rite of purification, the Lesser Banishing Rite of the Pentagram. The form given here is in *Hebrew*, but in the appendices you will find the Egyptian and Enochian versions.

The Banishing Ritual

Face east, and touch forehead, heart, right shoulder, and left shoulder, saying: "*ateh, malkuth, ve geborah, veh gedulah*" ("*Mine is the Kingdom, the Power, and the Glory*").

Cross your hands over your heart, saying *"le orlam, amen"* (*"Forever, Amen"*). This is a traditional statement of intent to purify. Still facing east, draw a banishing earth pentagram:

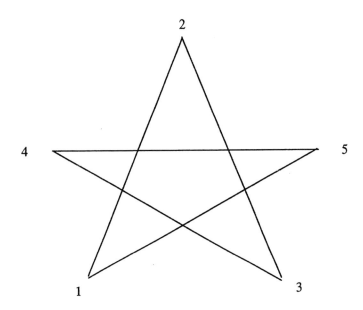

and say IHVH (*"yehowah"*) as you stab the centre. Draw a quarter circle, until you are facing south, where you draw another pentagram and say *adonai* as you stab the centre. Draw the quarter circle to the west, draw the pentagram and say AHI (*"ehieh"*) as you stab.

Finally, draw the quarter circle to the north, draw the pentagram and say AGLA (*"argle-ahh"*). The circle is now cast. Face east, with arms outstretched, and say:*"before me, raphael"* (*"Ra-fay-ell-ah"*: visualise a tall figure in yellow and purple robes)*"behind me, gabriel"* (*"Gah-bree-ell-ah"*:

visualise a tall figure in green and blue robes)*"on my right, michael"* ("Mee-kay-ell-ah": visualise a tall figure in red and orange robes)*"on my left, uriel"* *("ur-ee-ell-ah":* visualise a tall figure in citrine, olive, russet, and black)The Watchtowers are now present. *"for about me flames the pentagram"* (Visualise all you have drawn*)"and above me shines the six-rayed star"* (visualise a six-pointed star above your head) Finish with the Qabalistic Cross that you opened with, and you are done.

Homework

Practice the Banishing Ritual, recording results and impressions.

Chapter 21

Festivals

Theory

Through countless ages man has felt the need to celebrate the passing of the seasons and the months. In temperate regions the seasons' beginnings and ends are quite marked, and the Nature Mysteries have embodied the essence of the energy forms present in the times of seasonal change in the legends of the Triple Goddess and the Sacrificed King.

In Egypt the main seasonal events are the flooding of the Nile (the Inundation) and the cycle of Sirius. These events, and their attendant ones of sowing the seed, harvest, etc., provided occasions for celebrating events from the legends of the major deities.

Naturally, transferring these festivals to a country far from their origin poses certain problems. S.H.O.A.R has elected to celebrate festivals that have parallels in Europe on or around the appropriate European date, and to retain others at roughly the original dates.

There are nine regular Lodge meetings a year, and each one celebrates part of one of the legends.

March

The March meeting celebrates the Festival of Isis, specifically the conception of Horus, an appropriate subject for the month of the Spring Equinox.

April

Thoth's wisdom is celebrated this month, and it is also a popular month for initiations.

May

The legend of Shu and Tefnut and their part in the creation of the World is celebrated this month.

June

The legend of Isis and Ra is central to Egyptian Magick, and is celebrated in the month of the Summer Solstice.

July

Ra, as the Solar Logos, is fested in this, traditionally the warmest month in Britain.

August

With the heat of Ra, we are reminded of the time when he sent his daughter, Sekhmet, to punish mankind, so August is her month.

September

The Battle of Horus and Set is remembered here.

October

The month that ends with the Feast of the Dead for native pagans, when the world of men is closest to the realm of the Mighty Ones, it is appropriate to remember Anubis, Walker Between Worlds, Guide of the Dead, and Guardian of the Doorway to the Otherworld.

November

Since before history began, this is the month that saw the Festival of Osiris, celebrating his death and resurrection.

All of the festivals are celebrated in Lodge in addition to other work and initiations. There are also private rituals for members of the Order to practice alone or with partners.

Practical and homework

Look at the festivals and local feasts from Britain's pagan paths, and report on what you think are the reasons for the festivals being placed where they are.

Chapter 22

Symbolism

Theory

What are symbols, and why are they used in magick? These are two questions that are rarely asked, let alone answered, in many groups, covens, and Temples.

Basically, there are three types of symbol, but they all have one function: to convey in visual terms a concept, idea, or representation of an energy form.

The first type of symbol is the most common one, and is the symbol constructed using mathematical and/or geometrical concepts that mirror the spiritual concepts. A universal example is the pentagram, representing the elements in man, or the triangle representing the divine trinity of Father, Mother, and Son.

The second type is called a fetish by historians and is a stylised representation of an animal, tool, or other object sacred to a deity due to its association with that deity. An example is the crescent moon of the Great Mother, the horns of Cernunnos, the column of Osiris, the winged staff of Mercury, and the lightning bolt of Zeus. Some symbols fall into both of these categories, such as the Ankh, symbolising life, which is made up from a Tau cross and a circle, and can be seen as the sandal-strap of the Priest.

The final type of symbol is more correctly called the sigil. It is a design formed in some way from the name or statement relevant to what is being done. A famous example is the *abracadabra* triangle, or the fish of the early christians (used because the Greek letters standing for *"Jesus Christ God and Man"* spelt the Greek word Icthos, or fish). Symbols created by linking the letters of a name on a magical square, or the Hermetic Rose Cross lamen, fall into this category, as do the symbols in the manner used by Austin Osman Spare, where the letters themselves were manipulated into abstract form.

Practical

The easiest way of forming a symbol is by using the method of A.O. Spare, and can be used for either names or statements of intent. An example of each is given:

Statement:	*I want a good job*
Eliminate repeated letters:	*I want god jb*
Mix the letters:	*Ibwjadnotg*
Use them to form sigil:	*See illustration at end of lesson*
Name:	*Anubis*
Mix the letters:	*Asniub*
Use them to form sigil:	*See illustration at end of lesson*

These are ideal for use in talismans, but tend to be a little complex for visualisation without physical reminders.

Homework

Construct a talisman using the A.O. Spare system to create symbols for your name, a relevant deity, a statement of intent, a time period (eg.,THREE DAYS), and a key word (eg., luck, money). Place the sigils in a pentagram within a circle. Record the stages of development.

Chapter 23

Development of the Egyptian System

Theory

The story of the Egyptian Mysteries begins at the dawn of time, and has many aspects. Perhaps the easiest part of the story to uncover is the history of religion in the Land of Khem, and it is this aspect that will be examined here. If you choose to undertake further study within S.H.O.A.R, in later lessons you will learn about the spiritual evolution and the cosmic influences behind the historical facts, but it is important to be aware of all parts of the whole.

At the time of the coronation of Menes, the first recorded Pharaoh, Egypt was already a civilised land, rich in culture and material treasures, and much of what is considered typically Egyptian was already in place. What happened prior to that is not discernable from archaeological evidence, but legends suggest that the savage cannibalistic inhabitants of the Nile Valley were educated by an influx of people *"from the west"*, who taught them agriculture, law, astronomy, mathematics, and magick. More than one eminent scholar has expressed the opinion that it is as if the civilisation sprang up overnight.

The legends supporting this are, of course, those of Osiris, Isis, Ra and Horus, and many occultists see in these legends a memory of immigrants from Atlantis. Others see evidence of visits from Sirius in these legends, and indeed the star Sept or Sothis, as it was known to the Egyptians, was the focal point of many rituals and esoteric practices, in addition to being the subject of secret documents that contained information of staggering accuracy, such as the existence of Sirius B, the twin sun of the system that is only detectable with a radio telescope.

Whichever version you take - be they Atlanteans, alien visitors, or gods in the traditional sense - the teachers of this ancient time were deified and their archetypes became the embodiment of certain cosmic forces.

All of the gods of Egypt were originally local gods, perhaps even personal family gods or ancestors, that became national property as the Mysteries developed. Perhaps the oldest deities to be universally recognised were Sekhmet and Ptah - both are said to have been ancient when the world was created.

But perhaps the most significant group is that of Osiris, Isis, Set, Nephthys, and their families. Originating in Abydos, they became the royal family of the gods, and their Mystery was enlarged as they absorbed the legends and attributes of lesser deities who were seen as aspects of themselves.

As time went by the priests came to the realisation that as the local deities could be seen as aspects of the major deities, so they in turn could be perceived as aspects of the One True Creator, the Hidden One. This realisation enabled the priests to work together rather than in competition, and the great hierarchy of the temples and priesthoods came into being, evolving ever more complex and profound interpretations of the legends, weaving them into a Mystery of depth and beauty never seen before or since.

At the head of this hierarchy was the College of Six, a group of the highest ranking adepts in the land under the nominal leadership of the Pharaoh in his aspect of Incarnation of Horus. According to masonic tradition the founder of the College was Ases-Ra, and they were concerned with the evolution of the Mysteries and the governing of the Priesthood.

Next in line was an organisation known as the Four Orders, to which every senior priest of the temples belonged, and which was known to its members as the Noble Order of the Followers of Horus.

The more common name, the Four Orders, alluded to its division into four sections, typified by the deities Sekhmet, Thoth, Horus, and Isis, or by the four sons of Horus - representing the elements - after which it was named, which represented the four main approaches to spiritual and magical study.

The priests themselves were organised into a hierarchy of grades. A newly initiated priest was termed an Uab or We'eb priest, whose main concern was the maintenance of the Temple - cleaning and other menial tasks - and learning by observation.

The Hem Neter, or *"Servant of the God"*, studied more advanced topics, taught the Uabs, and assisted in the preparation and practice of the temple rites. The Hem Neter Tepy, or *"First Servant of the God"*, was a High Priest or High Priestess, of which there would be several - usually four - in each temple, being governed by a senior one. Their work was to officiate in the rites and ensure that all the priests were trained well. They were the lowest grade admitted to the Four Orders.

The Kher Heb priests were the adepts, who performed the Inner Mysteries, and attended to the religious needs of the Pharaoh and the Royal House. Not attached to a particular temple, they were accorded the status of hereditary princes of Abydos and governed particular groups of temples, either by region or devotion - being either the head of an Order serving a particular deity, or High Priest of a city or Nome.

Finally there were the Sen priests, who dealt specifically with the rituals that surrounded the Pharaoh. The Sen Priest or Priestess was seen as the supreme authority in spiritual matters, and would often represent the Pharaoh in rites that he could not attend personally.

There was one temple that was unusual, in that its officers were all Kher Heb priests, and that was the temple complex at Abydos. This Temple has seven sanctuaries instead of the usual single one, and each had its own High Priest. Behind the Sanctuary of Ra-Herachty (the exoteric, or outer, representation of Asar-Ra) lies a set of chambers, accessible from the sanctuary of Osiris, in which the Highest Mysteries of the Four Orders and the College of Six were performed. This Temple was the most sacred place in the world to the Egyptians, and was the headquarters of the whole of the Egyptian Mysteries.

One of the legends written at Abydos is about the end of the world. It states that after the end, all that will remain are the twin souls of Osiris and Ra, which combine to form *"Osiris in Ra, Ra in Osiris"*, who says,

"All that exists shall return into the Nun (Void). Myself alone, I remain, unknown, invisible to all."

The significance of this legend applies to the development of the Mysteries, for when the sacred world of the Land of Khem was spiritually destroyed by the conquering of Egypt by the Greeks, Romans, and Arabs, the only portion to remain were the cults of Ra and Osiris, which grouped under the banner of the Mysteries of Isis and spread throughout the world.

At the same time the Four Orders continued as an *"Invisible Order"*, both as a few adepts passing on their knowledge, and as an entity on the Astral. With the forced adoption of the Moslem faith in the Seventh century AD however, the material aspect of the Order was removed, the last Grand Master being Edfu-Amen-Ankh, who died without a successor. From that time on, although contact was occasionally made with the *"Invisible Order"*, and careful perusal of esoteric writing through the ages shows rare mentions of the Noble Order of the Followers of Horus, there was no organised material Order. The work of the Egyptian Mysteries was mostly carried out from the astral realms, and sometimes with groups sympathetic to the Egyptian Mysteries, such as the Masonic Rites of Memphis and Misraim, the Rosicrucian-type orders, and the Hermetic Order of the Golden Dawn.

In 1983, something happened. A young man, steeped in occult practices and initiated into Wicca, made contact with two entities on the Higher Planes, and in a vision was taken to the Hall of Truth where he underwent the Weighing of the Heart, and returned to the physical to begin several years of work to recover the system which he had been shown. The entities were Edfu-Amen-Ankh, last

Grand Master of the Four Orders, and Amenemta, who was High Priest of Ra at Abydos, architect of the Temple at Abydos and Thebes, and Chief of Works to the Pharaoh. Both had provided information about their life that was later verified. The system recovered became the rituals of S.H.O.A.R, and the exchange of information continues, as it is promised to continue for many years to come.

Chapter 24

The Astral Planes

am-tuat - The Astral Planes

Heaven

Upper Spiritual

Lower Spiritual

Upper Mental

Lower Mental

Upper Astral - Magical work

Lower Astral - Etheric Plane

EARTH

These levels all overlap at the edges. If we take Spiritual as one level, then there are five Planes, equating to the five subtle bodies used in the Egyptian Mysteries.

Material level to Astral:

Leave behind the physical body and physical sensations. The region of Action.

Astral level to Mental:

Leave behind the Astral body and the emotions. The region of learning.

Mental level to Spiritual:

Leave behind the ego and become your Higher Self. The region of Enlightenment.

The above diagram shows how the initiates of the Temples saw the astral realms divided. It appears to show them as layers, one on top of the other, but this is due to the limitations of a two-dimensional representation on paper. In reality, the planes are all superimposed on each other, occupying the same *"space"*.

The thing that makes one level *"higher"* than another is its rate of vibration. Just as the rate of vibration of energy rises as it becomes more subtle, more spiritual, so the astral realms operate on higher rates of vibration than lower planes.

All planes, including the physical, coexist here and now. In order to gain access to one or other of the astral planes, or am-tuat as the Egyptians called them, you must alter your perceptions so that you can perceive the relevant energies. The Egyptians did this by visualising an appropriate astral body in which they could travel in the desired realm. In practical terms, this meant raising the vibrations of your consciousness to match that of the realm you wish to visit.

It is important to remember that the realms are not cut and dried, with clearly marked borders. Just as the rate of energy vibration is a smoothly increasing scale, so is the energy that forms these realms. The splitting up into levels is quite arbitrary and artificial, used purely as a practical device that enables us to target a particular state of being.

There are several techniques that are used to visit these realms, the best known being astral projection. But a good pathworking also enables us to visit the astral realms, and lucid dreaming - itself a technique learnt on the way to developing astral projection - places the student squarely within the astral realms.

Chapter 25

Temple Etiquette

This chapter lays out general guidelines for attendance in a S.H.O.A.R lodge. The information is provided as an example of the sort of requirements that all ceremonial lodges insist upon, though the details given here are obviously specific to S.H.O.A.R You may use them as a model on which to build your own temple's etiquette, or simply as an example of the level of conformity required in High Magick. Naturally, personal ritual work is much less restricted as far as dress is concerned, but the level of commitment is still the same.

Attendance

Attendance at a Temple is a privilege of members of first degree and above, but is at the discretion of the Master of the Lodge concerned. Those who do well enough in this degree to qualify for initiation into the Priesthood may attend a Lodge by right.

When you attend a Lodge meeting, you must establish your right to be there before the start of the ritual - the Officer of the South will only admit those known to him/her and those vouched for by the Master, so you must present yourself, with your degree certificate and/or initiation certificate, to the Master, who will notify the OF of your right to attend.

Entering The Temple

On being admitted by the Officer of the South, walk straight to the altar, incline your head, and acknowledge the symbolism on it, then walk directly to a seat. You will usually be told who to sit next to. Make sure that you have the correct robe, etc.

Dress

All those attending a rite should wear the standard white robe with elbow-length sleeves, round neck and no hood. White temple shoes or sandals should be worn, and the appropriate cord and headdress.

Those not of the Priesthood should wear a black cord with a bead at each end for each degree passed, their degree lamen, and a white nemyss. They are referred to as Brother or Sister.

Members of the Priesthood wear identical attire to the non-initiates, but the degree lamen is on a red cord instead of a black one. But on special occasions they wear full regalia as follows.

Members of the first grade, Uabs, dress as usual, but may wear a red cord instead of a black one. They are referred to as the Honoured Uab NN.

Members of the second grade, Hem Neters, wear a cord in the colour appropriate to their patron deity, with the correct number of beads on each end. Those of appropriate degree wear the square apron. They are referred to as the Honoured Hem Neter NN.

Third grade members, Hem Neter Tepys, wear sash and apron of correct colour, and the fifth degree lamen. Those chosen as Special Envoys many wear their cloaks. They are referred to as the Greatly Honoured Hem Neter Tepy NN.

The Lodge Master will wear the same as other third grade members, except he/she will wear the ceremonial apron in the colour of the Lodge's patron Deity with the Lodge symbol upon it. Grand Lodge officers may wear a ceremonial apron in their patron Deity's colour with their cartouche upon it. At initiations the Master will wear the Red Crown, coloured either red or gold. He/she will wear the Master's Lamen, and carry the Lodge seal. He/she is referred to as the Most Honoured Hem Neter Tepy NN.

Titles

Apart from the formal titles above, used in rituals and presentations, most members may be referred to as Brother NN or Sister NN, and the Lodge Master as Master NN.

General

It is important to remember that the rite itself is a serious occasion, but do not be afraid to enjoy the socialising before and after the rite - though do not drink too much alcohol before the rite, or you will be excluded from it! Even within the rite there are moments when you can relax and be less serious, but observe until you are aware of appropriate moments - they will vary from Lodge to Lodge.

Please note the use of the word *"Honoured"* in the various titles. This is the reverse of the term *"Honourable"* or *"Right Honourable"* used by politicians. It reflects the initiates sense of honour that they have been granted the privilege of the priesthood, and the more exalted the position, the more honoured they feel to have it given to them.

Appendix A:

Homework Notes

Chapter One

The sort of things that you will see in the pathworkings are objects, creatures and symbols that have some association with the element concerned. For example, you would expect to see birds in the element of air, and hear the sound of bells or the wind. Flowers are likely to be spring varieties, and symbols representative of communication and science may be present.

Chapter Two

You will probably find that air and fire circles are the easiest ones to sense, unless you have a particular affinity with earth or water. With practice, most of the difficulties you may experience with one or more types of circle will go, and you will find all of your circles are stronger - both for the practice and for the elemental balance you will have developed.

Your circle essay should include ideas along the lines of the circle being a set-apart space, with the circumference representing the manifest universe and the centre representing the creator, or at a more personal level, the circumference representing the world and the centre representing you. You might find it useful to touch on the symbol of the circle as never-ending, and the fact that the circumference cannot exist without the centre, and vice-versa. Be creative in your reasoning, and look beneath the surface of any ideas that come to light - there may be another one hidden there!

Chapter Three

If you follow the basic concepts given in the chapter, and then follow your heart, you will not go far wrong. Temple altars should have a symmetrical layout, but this is not essential for a shrine. Once you have a shrine and prayer that you are happy with, write down your feelings about it, and - should you actually set the shrine up and use the prayer - record what it feels like to use them.

Chapter Four

It is useful to practice sensing the energy from different objects by gathering together a collection of - for example - a potted plant, a crystal, a plastic object, an electronic device (eg., radio) and a small animal, such as a pet hamster or a cat. Practice sensing the energy given off by each one until you feel confident of what you are sensing, then get a partner to blindfold you and test you with them. Record your results. With practice you can become very accurate, and develop your energy-sensing ability at the same time.

The second exercise may take some time, as you will have to develop your senses if they are not already sensitive enough, but the effort will be worthwhile. Your ability to sense different types of energy will be the lynchpin of so much of your work that if you "make-do" here you could seriously impede your later progress. Take the time to get it right.

Chapter Five

The exercises in this chapter are important for several reasons. The visualisations and attitudes given for the headdress, star lamen and cube are an important part of assuming the magical persona prior to ritual, and help you to get in touch with your higher self. You may find it useful to devise similar exercises for the robe, cord, and magical ring, if you wear one.

Chapter Six

This pathworking is a modern version of one that was actually used in the temples of Ancient Egypt. It is capable of producing profound initiatory experiences when used properly, so it is worth persevering with on a regular basis in addition to other exercises. At first you will experience it as little more than a controlled daydream, but even here the symbolism is affecting your subconscious. By the time you are experiencing it on a deeper level, you will be primed to release the full force of its power. But beware, the danger of the *"glamour"* is all too real, and once you are experiencing deep results, I would recommend doing only one pathworking per week, of any sort.

Chapter Seven

You may find the exercises in this chapter affect you in different ways. One deity may seem to almost be there in the flesh, while with another you may just get impressions of emotions, scents, or just *"vibes"*. Do not worry, this is perfectly natural, and as with most exercises, the impressions will become stronger and clearer with practice.

Chapter Eight

Your notes on your three subjects should include a brief description of them, what you can sense from their aura, and how you would go about healing them. At this stage, do not actually do any healing, unless you are really confident or have an experienced healer at hand to monitor your efforts. Keep the colours you visualise pale and bright, and at worse you will do no harm. You do not need to tell the subjects that you are observing them, but if you decide to give them healing, they should be asked for permission first.

Chapter Nine

Remember that the key to success with candle magick lies in the ability to focus your desires or needs on the candle flame. It may be appropriate to work for the same thing three times, letting the candle burn down completely each time. Please only work for positive things - while negative work will bring results, it will also adversely affect your karma.

Chapter Ten

The notes you make here will be the basis of your own tables of correspondences, and if you are working in a particular system, it would be a good idea to start with the tables that can be found in the key books on that system.

For more general correspondences, try Crowley's 777 or the books by Scott Cunningham etc.

Your elemental rite should be simple and from the heart. Just look for an appropriate incense, a deity to call upon, a candle colour and/or a stone that corresponds to the work. Cast a circle, put them together with words from the heart, and there you have it, one elemental rite.

Chapter Eleven

You will find that meditating on the Ankh results in a great quantity of associated images, and a pathworking that uses the ankh as a doorway will provide a lot of symbolism that will take time to understand. This is why it is so important to record all your results immediately after an exercise, so that you do not lose something that might turn out to be useful in the future.

Chapter Twelve

Meditating on the symbol representing a deity is a less vivid, but more controllable way of finding out about a deity. You may find that some symbols have a particular resonance with you, and this may lead you to be drawn to the deity concerned. This is an example of being chosen, rather than selecting your patron deity.

Chapter Thirteen

This chapter and the previous one are very similar, but here you are looking at the actual image of the deity, rather than the symbol. While much of the symbolism should be the same, you will find clues about the nature of the deity in its image, whereas you will find only what it represents in the symbol.

Chapter Fourteen

An awareness of the energies in incense, and the power of your sense of smell to aid focussing will bring out a whole new level in your ritual work. If you find you enjoy experimenting with incense, get some recipe books and experiment with your own concoctions.

Chapter Fifteen

You can use your given name, or a circle name if you have one. It is important to be honest with yourself here, then you may find the exercise useful in pointing out areas you need to work on. This is exactly the same as meditating on a godname, and so it follows that if you have a personal symbol, you can meditate on that, or on your face, just as you did with the deity symbols and images.

Chapter Sixteen

There is no homework given in this chapter, though you might find it useful to research some of the history of magick, especially the famous figures such as St Germain, Eliphas Levi, Crowley, Mathers, and *"fictional"* characters such as Faustus and Simon Magus. There is an excellent novel by Eric Erricson called Master of the Temple which, while fiction, contains a lot of information about these matters, as well as being a wonderful magical moral tale.

Chapter Seventeen

Just like in martial arts, do not stop practising these techniques just because you have succeeded with them. Regular practice will strengthen your ability and improve your psychic reflexes. Plus, as with all of these exercises, regular practice will also improve your general psychic and sensory abilities.

Chapter Eighteen

Each of the exercises given are ones that - traditionally - on their own can lead to contact with your higher self if practised daily, even if no other spiritual exercises are used.

This makes them doubly useful for anyone who is actively studying the Mysteries. You should record what effect your external environment, health, etc., have on the exercises.

Chapter Nineteen

The important thing with this exercise is to really plumb the depths of your own being. In addition to referring to the traditional meanings of the symbol, look at what it means to you - how it affects you. Use it as a gateway for a pathworking, and see where it leads you. Once again, take your time and be thorough.

Chapter Twenty

The Lesser Ritual of the Banishing Pentagram is another ritual act that is said to bring enlightenment if practised by itself, and contains all of the elements of a good rite without being over-long. It is easy to memorise it in any of its forms, though naturally I would recommend the Egyptian form.

Chapter Twenty-one

It is important to be in tune with the seasonal changes around you, as all rites of a celebratory nature have links to certain events in the wheel of the year. The biggest mistake anyone can make with festivals is to try to adhere rigidly to a timetable meant for another country.

Chapter Twenty-two

The sigils created by the Spare system, and also the systems such as the Hermetic Rose, may be considered almost to be modern hieroglyphs, and the thought and energy that goes into creating them makes them very potent. This is a simple yet effective form of talismanic magick that can be used on its own or in combination with more traditional elements of talisman design.

Chapter Twenty-three

Though there is no set homework for this lesson, you would benefit from meditating on the information put forward in this chapter, and forming your own conclusions concerning it. The information is naturally part of the S.H.O.A.R tradition, but much of it is based on ancient sources. It is for you to decide at what level the non-verifiable material can be considered true.

Chapter Twenty-four

The astral realms are where much of the work of the Egyptian Mysteries are carried out, so it is important to develop a facility for interacting with them. The exercise given is the start of a regime aimed at the attainment of full astral projection, and it is purely a matter of the individual's natural ability that decides how long the process takes.

Chapter Twenty-five

When entering someone's sacred place, it is polite to show respect for their beliefs, and this is best accomplished by observing the etiquette associated with the place - eg., removing head coverings (for males) in a Christian church, and covering the head when entering a synagogue. Most of the etiquette in esoteric temples and lodges are based in practical considerations to do with energy-flow, so you should always enquire - if not told - how to behave when visiting a group. Based on the other chapters in this book, you should be able to work out the practical motives for the etiquette given in this chapter, and this would be a worthwhile exercise.

Appendix B

Banishing Ritual - Enochian

The following rite is taken from Gerals Scheuler's book
Enochian Magick, published by Llewellyn. In the centre of
the temple/room, face east and perform the Pentagram
upon yourself by touching the following points in order and
saying the words:

Forehead	**Zoh-ah**	*"Mine is"*
Left nipple	**Oh-en-doh**	*"The Kingdom"*
Right Shoulder	**Mee-heh**	*"The Power"*
Left shoulder	**Boo-Zoh-dee**	*"The Glory"*
Right nipple	**Pah-ee-deh**	*"Forever"*

then touch forehead again.

Trace the pentagram towards the east as in the Qabalistic
version, and say:

    Et-zar-peh   *"Air"*

Trace the pentagram towards the south as in the Qabalistic
version, and say:

    Bee-toh-meh   *"Fire"*

Trace the pentagram towards the west as in the Qabalistic version, and say:

Heh-koh-meh *"Water"*

Trace the pentagram towards the north as in the Qabalistic version, and say:

Nah-en-tah *"Earth"*

Remain facing North, stand with arms outstretched, and say:

> *"Before me, Ee-keh-zod-hee-kal*
> *Behind me, Eh-del-par-nah-ah*
> *On my right, Bah-tah-ee-vah-heh*
> *On my left, Ra-ah-gee-oh-sel*
> *Behold the four flaming Pentagrams, and I alone in*
> *the centre".*

The Enochian words are spelt phonetically. Visualisations are as for the qabalistic version, but the four figures named in the end speech should be visualised seated on huge stone thrones.

Appendix C

Lesser Banishing Ritual - Egyptian Version

Standing in the centre, face east and perform the Qabalistic Cross, using the following words:

Forehead -	**Pai-a**	*"Mine"*
	("Pay-ah")	
Sternum -	**Sutenit**	*"The Kingdom"*
	("Sootenit")	
Right shoulder -	**Hekau**	*"The Power"*
	("Heh-cow")	
Left shoulder -	**Auah aui**	*"And The Glory"*
	("OwahOwee")	
Crossed hands -	**m au-t tchet**	*"For Eternity"*
	("um ow-t chet")	

Trace the pentagram towards the east as in the Qabalistic version, and say:

> **Qebhsnuf** *("Kwebsnuff")*   Son of Horus who rules Air

Trace the pentagram towards the south as in the Qabalistic version, and say:

161

Duamutef *("Doo-am-oo-teff")*   Son of Horus who rules
Fire

Trace the pentagram towards the west as in the Qabalistic version, and say:

Imsety *("Im-set-ee")*   Son of Horus who rules Water

Trace the pentagram towards the north as in the Qabalistic version, and say:

Hapi *("Har-pee")*   Son of Horus who rules Earth

Face east and stand with arms outstretched, saying:

Serket *("Ser-ket")*   Tutelary Goddess of the East
Neith *("Neeth")*   Tutelary Goddess of the South
Isis   Tutelary Goddess of the West
Nephthys *("Neff-thiss")* Tutelary Goddess of the North

Tut en Asar-Ra em aq hati-a
("Toot en Ass-ar Ra emm akk hattee-ah")
("With an image of Asar-Ra in the middle of my breast")
Amma tu erta-na Hekau
("Amm-ah too ert-ah-nah Heh-cow")
("Grant that I may be given Words of Power")

Then repeat the qabalistic cross as above.

Appendix D

Casting a Circle

Anyone who has been taught about circle-casting and ritual construction can create their own Egyptian rites, but for those who are new to magick, or do not have the time to create their own rituals, I am including here the method of opening and closing the circle as used by S.H.O.A.R., and some guidelines on formulating a ritual.

It is important to remember that you should never perform a magickal act without first understanding why you are doing it and what it means. It may appear that I am stating the obvious, but if you look through the Greek Magical Papyrae, you will come across rites that seem safe, useful and are designed to do positive things, but which contain invocations to dark aspects of deities: such invocations could have grave repercussions on your life. Unless, that is, you know how to handle them.

"Barbarous Words of Power" are used in many ancient rites. These are not so much words as sonic vibrations that have profound psychological effects on our subconscious, and even greater magical effect on the Astral Plane. It is not a good idea to use them in your rites unless you have access to someone who can train you to intone them correctly and warn you of probable effects. For all practical purposes, the names of the deities, properly vibrated and projected, will

more than suffice. This, then, is the script of the S.H.O.A.R. Lodge Ritual in full. After it you will find an explanation of all parts of it. It is written to be performed by four people, conventionally referred to as officers of the quarters, but can be performed by two, or even by solo practitioners. If more than four people take part, then the extras are non-speaking participants, but should still actively participate by willing their energies to the speakers. They may also join in when *"So mote it be"* is said.

Officer of the North silently draws the circle three times with sword, dagger or fingers, visualising a line of blue light streaming forth as he/she does so. He/she then opens portal and admits the others, if any. Officer of the North: (Osiris Litany)

> *Praise and songs of glory unto thee, o osiris, un-nefer, lord of the hidden place, whose form is majestic. Be thou in my heart, o bringer of harvest, and inspire thou me to works of truth and beauty in thine honour. Great is thy form, and wise are thy words, o lord of the two rivers. thy servant waiteth, and is but an empty vessel to be filled with thy luminescence. Breathe thou into him that divine inspiration that causeth the earth to rock on its foundations, o thou who art endless light.*

(Isis Litany)

> *In the beauty of the night sky I behold thee, o isis, and my heart is light with thy presence. O thou who art consort to thy brother, the lord of all, I do bow to thy beauty, and honour thee with every act of love. Quietly as a lark's whisper to the setting sun do I hear thy*

words in my mind, fair goddess, and my very soul is filled with rapture at thy touch. Be thou the governess of my emotions, that I may love and serve thee and thy husband, osiris of the one face, with the purity of perfect truth.

All face East

Officer of the East:

Mighty qebhsnuf, son of horus, lord of air, we do greet thee and ask thy attendance and assistance in this rite.

All:

So mote it be!

All face South

Officer of the South:

Mighty duamutef, son of horus, lord of fire, we do greet thee and ask thy attendance and assistance in this rite.

All:

So mote it be!

All face West

Officer of the West:

Mighty imsety, son of horus, lord of water, we do greet thee and ask thy attendance and assistance in this rite.

All:
So mote it be!
All face North.

Officer of the North:

Mighty hapi, son of horus, lord of earth, we do greet thee and ask thy attendance and assistance in this rite.

All:
So mote it be!

All face Altar.

Officer of the North: (Osiris invocation)

Hail, thou lord of the sacred lands, thou majestic one of the underworld! strengthen thou us according as thou hast strengthened thyself, and show thyself upon the earth, o thou that returnest and withdrawest thyself, and let thy will be done!

(Isis invocation)

Great isis, behold, thy handmaiden waits for thy presence. make her thy garment for a short space of time. May thy blood, and thy powers,and thy enchantments be in her, that she may do thy work in this place.

Officer of the East: (Osiris invocation)

Behold, the god of one face is with me. I am the hawk that is within the shrine, and I open that which is upon the hangings thereof. Behold osiris, triumphant in glory!

(Isis invocation)

I am she who bore the child horus! I am she who knows the secret name of ra. Learn the deepest secret of this universe, and you will find me in it. The queen of magick is at the heart of all things, and I am she. Behold isis, great goddess of mystery!

Then follows any work to be done, followed by the Close. Officer of the East:

The time has come for an ending - for all things must end, that there may be a new beginning. But remember ye this - the light of the temple burns in the heart of us all, thus are we all temples of light and must deport ourselves accordingly.

All face East

Officer of the East:

Mighty qebhsnuf, son of horus, lord of air, we thank thee for thy presence, and bid thee return to thy abode in peace.

All:
So mote it be!

All face South

Officer of the South:

Mighty duamutef, son of horus, lord of fire, we thank thee for thy presence and bid thee return to thy abode in peace.

All:
So mote it be!

All face West

Officer of the West:

Mighty imsety, son of horus, lord of water, we thank thee for thy presence and bid thee depart to thy abode in peace.

All:
So mote it be!

All face North

Officer of the North:

> *Mighty hapi, son of horus, lord of earth, we thank thee for thy presence and bid thee depart to thy abode in peace.*

All:
> *So mote it be!*

All face Altar

Officer of the North:

> *All that has been created shall return into the nun. . . Myself alone, I remain, unknown, invisible to all.*

Officer of the East:

> *In the name of the lord of all, I now set free any spirits that may have been trapped by this ceremony.*

The Officer of the North claps his hands once.

Officer of the North:

> *The rite is ended!*

All:
> *So mote it be!*

Preparation

The circle is prepared with an altar, preferably square, in the centre. At each Quarter is a chair for the officer, with the Quarter candle to its left: seats for other participants may be placed around the perimeter of the room. The candle colours conform to the colours for the Sons of Horus as given below.

On the Altar should be two altar candles, an oil lamp and a representation of the deity to be worked with; either a statue, a picture, or the deity's symbol. Other relevant items may be added, but this is a comfortable minimum. The participants should all wear plain white robes with black cords if they are initiated, and white cords if they are not initiated into any system. Temple shoes are optional, but if worn, should be used exclusively for Egyptian rituals. Daggers should be worn on the cord if required.

The Litany

If the Officer of the East is male, the Osiris Litany and invocation are used; if female, the Isis litany and invocation are used. The litany is used for two purposes. Firstly, it helps to get everyone in the right frame of mind for the ritual, and gives a chance to calm down and open up. Secondly, it traditionally notifies the deity that he or she will be called upon, a sort of courtesy call. If deities other than Osiris or Isis are used you can write or find an appropriate litany to use, but for beginners and for most works of healing, learning and helping, Osiris and Isis will work perfectly well.

Sons of Horus

These are the Lords of the Four Quarters in the Egyptian System. In this rite they are placed in the quarters that S.H.O.A.R. associates them with, but different authorities give other placements. The table below gives the basic details needed for working with them;

Name	Pronounced	Element	Quarter	Head	Colour
Qebhsnuf	Kwebs-nuf	Air	East	Hawk	Blue
Duamutef	Doo-amoo-tef	Fire	South	Jackal	Red
Imsety	Imm-settee	Water	West	Human	Green
Hapi	Har-pee	Earth	North	Baboon	Yellow

When you speak the words that summon one of the Sons of Horus, draw an invoking pentagram: either the pentagram of the relevant element, or the invoking earth pentagram illustrated - and visualise a kilted man with the appropriate head of the appropriate colour standing before you.

Invocation

Obviously, the invocation to match the initial litany is used. The invocation is in two parts, one said by the Officer of the North, and the other by the Officer of the East, who is the celebrant. All present should visualise the Officer of the East growing larger until he is so tall that the planet earth is a footstool on which he or she stands. They should then visualise him or her merging with the deity being invoked, and shrinking back down, bringing the deity into the circle, where the second part of the invocation is said to establish the presence of the deity.

The Work

In the temples of Ancient Egypt, most work was done using thought-forms, astral projection, and the spoken word. The use of wax effigies and talismans was more of a solo practice. The real key to the magick is visualisation, and the most basic - but still effective - form of visualisation is to picture the relevant deity supervising an event where the desired outcome takes place.

A table of practical uses for the deities is given below, but don't forget to thank the gods both after the work, and again when the result is obtained. They like to be thanked as much as we mortals do, and your magick will be more effective if you remember this.

Godform	Appropriate rites.
Ra	Money, good fortune, protection, strength.
Osiris	Farming, gardening, law courts, justice, healing of the body.
Isis	Healing of the mind, protection (especially of children) gaining magickal knowledge, oracles.
Horus	Strength, healing, righting a wrong, protection.
Set	To bring rain and/or wind, works of destruction, facing your own negative aspects.
Nephthys	Things of the sea, secrets, protection, aiding the passage through death.

Anubis	Travel, protection, finding lost things, healing oracles.
Hathor	Music, dance, love, healing by purging, preventative medicine, protection.
Sekhmet	Passion, strength, authority, healing, learning.
Ptah	Buildings, plans, arts and crafts, oracles.
Thoth	Books, information, science, healing, communication.
Asar-Ra	Spiritual development, union with Higher Self

If you are unsure of which one to use, meditate on the problem.

The Close

Just as the circle must be opened at the start, it must be closed at the end, and this is done in a very straightforward manner. The Officers use the banishing pentagrams, and as the Officer of the East says *"The rite is ended"*, he claps his hands together once, loudly.

Initiate of S. H. O. A. R.

Appendix E

Shai en Hekau - the Rituals of S.H.O.A.R

The following are a selection of rituals used within S.H.O.A.R that may be useful for you if you wish to practice Egyptian magick. Some rites, such as the Rite of Dedication, are designed for group use - though they can, of course, be adapted for solo use - but others are designed for the solo magician.

Rite of Dedication

This rite is to enable the student to make a commitment to the Mysteries before they are ready for initiation. It also involves consecration in the four Elements, which is designed to give your studies a boost, and sets you apart as one who is dedicated to the Egyptian Mysteries. To convert to solo use, just reword everything to say yourself, or leave it as it is and visualise the other participants.

The Rite

Cast circle as in Appendix D, then the candidate is brought before the Celebrant.

Celebrant:	*What do you wish?*
Candidate:	Open unto me!
Celebrant:	*Who then art thou?*
Candidate:.	I am a human being, an Anemu, who would be one with you.
Celebrant:	*What is thy name?*
Candidate:	(gives name)
Celebrant:	*Let there be given unto me vessels of milk, together with cakes, and loaves of bread, and cups of drink, and pieces of meat in the Temple. Grant thou me these things wholly?*
Candidate:	Let it so be done that I may enter in like a hawk, and that I may come forth like the Bennu Bird, and like the Morning Star. Let me make my path so that I may go in peace into the beautiful Amentet, and let the Lake of Osiris be mine. Let me make my path, and let me enter in, and let me adore Osiris, the Lord of Life.
Celebrant:	*Art thou willing to dedicate thyself to the pursuit of the Hidden Knowledge?*
Candidate:	I am
Celebrant:	*Then proclaim thy dedication!*

Candidate: I (name) do this day solemnly promise and
               swear before thee, O Osiris, and before the
               Sons of Horus, that with the divine
               permission I will from this day forward apply
               myself to the Great Work, which is so to
               purify and exalt my spiritual nature that
               with the divine aid I may at length attain to
               be more than human, and thus gradually
               right and raise myself to myhigher and
               divine genius, and that in this event I will
               not abuse the great power entrusted unto
               me. I further solemnly pledge myself not to
               debase my knowledge of practical magick to
               purposes of evil. Lords of the four Quarters,
               witness this my solemn oath!

The Candidate kneels before the Celebrant

Celebrant: *I consecrate thee with Air in the name of
               Osiris Un-Nefer, the Justified One, and
               invoke the powers of Qebhsnuf, Son of Horus,
               Lord of Air, that you may be protected and
               guided by his Kerubs.*

All: So mote it be!

Celebrant: *I consecrate thee with Fire in the name of
               Osiris Un-Nefer, the Justified One, and
               invoke the powers of Duamutef, Son of Horus,
               Lord of Fire, that you may be protected and
               guided by his Kerubs.*

All: So mote it be!

Celebrant:	*I consecrate thee with Water in the name of Osiris Un-Nefer, the Justified One, and invoke the powers of Imsety, Son of Horus, Lord of Water, that you may be protected and guided by his Kerubs.*
All:	So mote it be!
Celebrant:	*I consecrate thee with Earth in the name of Osiris Un-Nefer, the Justified One, and invoke the powers of Hapi, Son of Horus, Lord of Earth, that you may be protected and guided by his Kerubs.*
All:	So mote it be!
Celebrant:	*In the name and power of the Divine Spirit I invoke ye, ye Lords of the Watchtowers of the Universe. Guard this Brother/Sister during his/her life. Keep far from him/her that which is evil, and inspire and sanctify him/her with the illimitable wisdom of the Light Devine.*
All:	So mote it be!
Celebrant:	*Brother/Sister (name), I welcome you as an Anemu of the Sacred Hermetic Order of Asar-Ra, known of old as the Noble Order of the Followers of Horus, and as Ser Neter Sa en Asar-Ra in the Ancient land of Khem. Ankh! Utah! Semb!*
All:	Life! Strength! Health! So mote it be!

Consecration of the Magical Ring

This rite is taken from an ancient magical papyrus. It contains *"Barbarous Words of Power"* that have been written out phonetically to aid pronunciation. The ring should be of silver or gold, with a crystalline stone set in it. Amethyst - sacred to Thoth - is particularly good in a magical ring.

Preliminary

Place a container of Myrrh oil or Temple oil in the centre of the altar, surrounded by olive leaves (bay leaves). Burn myrrh and Khyphi incense on the altar. Charge the oil with golden-white energy, and place the ring in it. Leave the ring in the oil for three days.

The Rite

After the three days are up, cast the circle and open in the usual way, then continue as follows. The Celebrant should be alone, unless the ring is for someone else, in which case that person may be present.

Invocation of Thoth

Celebrant:
> *I call to you, O Thoth, the Hearing-Ear, who
> listens to everything. I call you in the names
> which are great, which are divine; Ah-lee-pess thab-
> lee-pess sat-see-eel-ee-pess gah-gar-peh-oh-thar thah-
> nah-see-mah kwah or-thoh-men-kroon bal-sah ah-lah-
> bah-kah-bel. Awaken to me, O Lord of Truth!*

The Celebrant makes an offering of bread and fruit upon
the altar, and anoints his/her forehead with the oil, taking
the ring from the oil and putting it on.

Consecration

Celebrant:
> *I am Thoth, discoverer and founder of drugs and
> letters. Come to me, you under the Earth, arouse
> yourself for me, Great Osiris, Thou of Nun, the
> subterranean. I am the famous heron, egg of ibis, egg
> of the falcon, egg of the air-ranging phoenix, having
> under my tongue the mud of em, I wear the hide of
> Keph. May I know what is in the minds of everyone, of
> every race and people; may I know what has been and
> what shall be; may I know their skills, and their
> practices, and their works, and their friends, and their
> names, and their lives, even of those now dead.*

If the ring is for someone else, substitute their name for *"I"*
in the above. Close in the usual way.

The Rite of Thoth

This rite is used to celebrate the Festival of Thoth, and leads to a meditation on the deity.

The Rite

Open in the usual way. The Officer of the East then faces the initiate who is representing Thoth.

OE:

I call to you, O Thoth, the Hearing-Ear, who listens to everything. I call you in the names which are great, which are divine; Ah-lee-pess thab-lee-pess sat-see-eel-ee-pess gah-gar-peh-oh-thar thah-nah-see-mah kwah or-thoh-men-kroon bal-sah ah-lah-bah-kah-bel. Awaken to me, O Lord of Truth!

Thoth:

I am the Great God in the highest boat. I will fight for you. I am one among those gods who are the Divine Chiefs, and the Truth-Speaker for Osiris against his enemies on that day that is called the evaluation of words. I am with your devotees, O Osiris. I am with those gods born as the children of the goddess Nuit, who righteously slay the enemies of Osiris, and who close the doors of death for him. I am with your devotees, O Horus. I will fight for you. I have sent forth your name. I am Thoth, the Truth-Speaker for Osiris against his enemies on the day that is called the evaluation of words in the house of the Ancient One who dwells in Annu.

OE:

Mighty Thoth, we know you in your different forms, but their purpose is a mystery to us. Speak to us of your forms, that we may learn.

Thoth:

I am the God Thoth, the sacred ibis who has been since before the dawn of time. I guard the Great Egg wherefrom came Ra as he called the universe into being - I am that word, and I existed before it. In the sanctuary of my Temple I am the sacred ibis, the Living Word, and my power is the power of the Laws of the universe.

I am the God Thoth, the sacred Scribe of the Gods, who writes down all that occurs from the dawn of time to its end. I guard the sacred writings that only those who come in Truth may partake of my secret wisdom - I am that wisdom, and encompass all. In the sanctuary of my Temple I am the sacred Scribe, the written word, and my power is the power of the teachings of the Mystery.

I am the God Thoth, the dog-faced ape who testifies for mankind. I guard the knowledge that leads to enlightenment, giving initiation to those who deserve it - I am that initiation, and I am the initiated. In the sanctuary of my Temple I am the dog-faced ape, the intellect of man, and my power is the power of the knowledge of the Mystery.

OE:

Great Lord, reveal to us the mystery as we open ourselves to you.

Go into meditation chanting Ra-Ma as described in this book, followed by discussion and close.

Bibliography

The Goddess Sekhmet, Robert Masters, Amity

Egyptian Magic, C Jacq, Arris & Phillips

Occult Arts of Ancient Egypt, B Bromage, Aquarian

Egyptian Mysteries, Attrib. Iamblicus, Weiser

The Book of the Dead, Budge, Routledge & Kegan Paul

Osiris (2 vols), Budge, Dover

Egyptian Magic, Budge, Dover

Egyptian Scriptures Interpreted, G Gaskill, Theosophical

Dictionary of Egyptian Gods & Goddesses, G Hart, RKP

Practical Egyptian Magic, Murry Hope, Aquarian

Egypt: the Sirian Connection, Murry Hope, Element

Awakening Osiris, Ellis, Phanes

Sphinx & the Megaliths, John Ivimy, Turnstone

Ancient Egyptian Coffin Texts (3 vols), Faulkner, Arris & Phillips

Egyptian Myths, G Hart, British Museum

The Greek Magical Papyrae in Translation, Betz, Chicago

Coming Into the Light, G & B Scheuler, Llewellyn

The Splendour That Was Egypt, Margaret Murray, BCAA

Guide to Religious RituaL at Abydos, R Davis, Arris &
Phillips

Index

FREE DETAILED CATALOGUE

A detailed illustrated catalogue is available on request, SAE or International Postal Coupon appreciated. Titles are available direct from Capall Bann, post free in the UK (cheque or PO with order) or from good bookshops and specialist outlets. Title currently available include:

Animals, Mind Body Spirit & Folklore
Angels and Goddesses - Celtic Christianity & Paganism by Michael Howard
Arthur - The Legend Unveiled by C Johnson & E Lung
Auguries and Omens - The Magical Lore of Birds by Yvonne Aburrow
Book of the Veil The by Peter Paddon
Call of the Horned Piper by Nigel Jackson
Cats' Company by Ann Walker
Celtic Lore & Druidic Ritual by Rhiannon Ryall
Compleat Vampyre - The Vampyre Shaman: Werewolves & Witchery by Nigel Jackson
Crystal Clear - A Guide to Quartz Crystal by Jennifer Dent
Earth Dance - A Year of Pagan Rituals by Jan Brodie

Earth Magic by Margaret McArthur
Enchanted Forest - The Magical Lore of Trees by Yvonne Aburrow
Healing Homes by Jennifer Dent
Herbcraft - Shamanic & Ritual Use of Herbs by Susan Lavender & Anna Franklin
In Search of Herne the Hunter by Eric Fitch
Inner Space Workbook - Developing Counselling & Magical Skills Through the Tarot
Kecks, Keddles & Kesh by Michael Bayley
Living Tarot by Ann Walker
Magical Incenses and Perfumes by Jan Brodie
Magical Lore of Animals by Yvonne Aburrow
Magical Lore of Cats by Marion Davies

Magical Lore of Herbs by Marion Davies
Masks of Misrule - The Horned God & His Cult in Europe by Nigel Jackson
Mysteries of the Runes by Michael Howard
Oracle of Geomancy by Nigel Pennick
Patchwork of Magic by Julia Day
Pathworking - A Practical Book of Guided Meditations by Pete Jennings
Pickingill Papers - The Origins of Gardnerian Wicca by Michael Howard
Psychic Animals by Dennis Bardens
Psychic Self Defence - Real Solutions by Jan Brodie
Runic Astrology by Nigel Pennick
Sacred Animals by Gordon MacLellan
Sacred Grove - The Mysteries of the Forest by Yvonne Aburrow
Sacred Geometry by Nigel Pennick
Sacred Lore of Horses The by Marion Davies
Sacred Ring - Pagan Origins British Folk Festivals & Customs by Michael Howard
Secret Places of the Goddess by Philip Heselton
Talking to the Earth by Gordon Maclellan
Taming the Wolf - Full Moon Meditations by Steve Hounsome
The Goddess Year by Nigel Pennick & Helen Field
West Country Wicca by Rhiannon Ryall
Witches of Oz The by Matthew & Julia Phillips

Capall Bann is owned and run by people actively involved in many of the areas in which we publish. Our list is expanding rapidly so do contact us for details on the latest releases. We guarantee our mailing list will never be released to other companies or organisations.

Capall Bann Publishing, Freshfields, Chieveley, Berks, RG20 8TF